One of Canada's foremost writers, Hugh MacLennan was born in Nova Scotia. He was a Rhodes Scholar at Oriel College, Oxford, and later did research in Roman history at the Graduate College of Princeton. After some years of teaching school in Canada, he was able to devote his full time to writing: he has published four novels and two books of essays and he contributes frequently to Canadian magazines and to *Holiday*. Mr. MacLennan now teaches two courses in the English Department of McGill University.

Of his principal concern Mr. MacLennan has this to say: "I think the novel is still the subtlest and most accurate of all the literary forms invented, so long as it tells a story about real people and seeks to communicate and is written with a little love."

THE RIVERS OF CANADA

HUGH MACLENNAN

The Rivers of Canada

THE MACKENZIE

THE ST. LAWRENCE

THE OTTAWA

THE RED

THE SASKATCHEWAN

THE FRASER

THE ST. JOHN

CHARLES SCRIBNER'S SONS

New York

For Frances Aline, with my love

CONTENTS

INTRODUCTION

This is a book about one man's experience with seven major rivers of Canada. It grew out of a suggestion made to me several years ago by Ralph Allen, who then was editor of *Maclean's*, that I contribute a series of river pieces to the magazine. Over a period of two and a half years I did so, and it was a fascinating adventure in space and time.

Space – much of North American art and literature has been obsessed with it. How to use space in design, how to communicate its fullness, how to proportion human beings to it, how to reveal the effects of immense land horizons on the descendants of people whose traditions stem from little cities in Greece and neat countries like Italy, France, Holland and England – the artistic necessity here has been much more difficult than European critics ever seem to realize.

It was certainly the heart of my problem in writing about these Canadian rivers. They wind through forests and plains, they charge down mountain gorges, and most of the territory through which they pass is void of habitation. Space apparently boundless, and on the prairies without even the suggestion of a frame, but space not dead because those living currents flow through them. No assignment I ever undertook gave me such a sense of Canada's unique geography, or of the effect of that geography on her people. As I sailed on the rivers, as I flew over them, as I drove along their banks with my wife beside me, she seeing some of them for the first time and feeling the essence of her country for the first time, space became a living personality to me, and the rivers the pulse of its life.

Time also, that mysterious companion of space – as I grow older, and I suppose it is the same with us all, the past merges with the present and time becomes a continuum in my personal life. But in Canada the time-sense of the people was abruptly fractured when the railway age began. After the Hitler War, when nearly everyone took to the air, this still newer sense of time all but obliterated the nature of the original Canadian experience. In a vast country like Canada, space in our daily lives can only be measured by the time and expenditure of effort it takes people to cover it. This modern Canadian life has not grown out of us; it has been imposed on us by technology. That may be why the nation seems almost to have out-travelled its own soul. That may be why, for most of us, Canadian history has not so much become a dead thing as an unknown thing.

A knowledge of the Canadian rivers will recover this earlier sense of time in Canada. It will bring the old experience of the people out of the subconscious regions where it lies buried.

Before the railway age, the rivers were the sole means of communication in this country, and the use of them to overcome space produced a kind of man, the voyageur, whose courage and endurance were such that no modern man could believe that anyone ever lived like that were the evidence not so detailed and conclusive. The early Canadian experience can only be described by one word – epic. But though a few enthusiasts are still acquainted with it, and treasure an accurate knowledge of its details with the jealous love of connoisseurs, most Canadians today know nothing of it at all. This ignorance lies like a chasm between the modern Canadian and his ancestors. Today this fabulous past – and the over-worked word is really too weak to describe it – is virtually unknown save to a small body of professional historians.

I owe them much, yet it embarrasses me to acknowledge so late a debt to Harold Innis, Bartlet Brebner, Donald Creighton, Arthur S. Morton and various others whose work I read, and felt, while doing so, much as Keats did on first looking into Chapman's *Homer*. Had this story been here all this time and I ignorant of it? Why, I asked myself, did I wait for fifty years before I learned anything important about so many of the men who made possible the existence of the nation?

Well, I know something about them now, and it is better late than never. But I do not wish to imply that this little book of mine is history as Innis and the others understood the meaning of that word. It was never intended to be that. But to give a sense of the mystery, the beauty and the variety of our rivers, to indicate in passing how they link us with our past, and to do so in a series of semi-personal essays arising out of my own belated discovery of them – that is all the purpose I have here.

Originally, before going to the researches of the professional historians, I found, as other Canadians did, a few books about some of our rivers directed to the general reader. There was Bruce Hutchison's book on the Fraser, Leslie Roberts' on the Mackenzie, Esther Clark Wright's on the St. John. There were Marjorie Wilkins Campbell's *The Saskatchewan* and *The North West Company*. In *The Voyageur*, Grace Lee Nute had presented such a vivid and exciting picture of the early life on the Canadian rivers that I wished every high school student in the country had read her book. Behind all these books, moreover, were the journals of voyageurs, explorers and travellers from Champlain until the middle of the nineteenth century.

The essays I publish here are seldom in the form in which they appeared in *Maclean's*. Space requirements in the magazine forced me to abbreviate the earlier ones, so here I have re-written and enlarged them. The first two chapters are entirely new, and so is the one on the Mackenzie. That immense river of the north moved me strangely. It is the largest and the most majestic of them all, and the least known except to a handful of men who know its every shoal. Living on the Mackenzie, sailing down it day after day on a working tugboat, enables you to feel a little of what Canada was like in the days of the old time-sense when there were no railways or highways, and those winding, cold currents were the sole avenues of travel.

Finally, I would like to thank *Maclean's* for allowing me to reprint some of the material I sent them, and above all to thank Ralph Allen for having persuaded me to accept an assignment which became an intense personal experience.

Hugh MacLennan, Montreal, 1961

The Canadian River Systems 1

Years ago an American reviewer remarked that a novel of mine
had a Russian atmosphere; he said the book was pervaded by what
he called "a true northern melancholy". This he deduced not from
the lives of the characters, but from the effects on them of living
in a huge land far in the north.

At first his acceptance of the old stereotype annoyed me.
Canada, at least the parts of it where most of us live, is not
northern in terms of latitude. It is no land of midnight suns and
midday dusks. My home town of Halifax lies approximately on
the same meridian as Milan, and Windsor is almost as far south
as Rome. Even Lake Athabaska lies well to the south of Leningrad,
and Edinburgh is farther north than our most northerly large city.

But when I recalled the summer I spent in Scandinavia and
Russia before the war, it occurred to me that this American reviewer was probably right. Nearly all the moods of Canada can be
duplicated in Russia and in the Scandinavian regions. New Brunswick is very like Karelia, in the Laurentian forests a Swede would
feel completely at home, the British Columbia coastline has often
been compared to the fjords of Norway. Russia itself, at least so far
as the landscape goes, is more like central Canada than any other
country on earth. The civilized portions of Canada may not be
northern in terms of latitude, but climatically they are, and also in
appearance, because of three phenomenons of nature from which
Europeans are exempt. One of these is the permanent ice cap on
Greenland, another is the permanent ice cover on the Canadian
polar sea, the third is that the results of the Ice Ages are visible in
the western hemisphere much farther south than in the eastern.

The effect wrought on the Canadian climate by the huge refrig-
erators on Greenland and the Polar Sea is peculiar: they make
eastern Canada much colder, in proportion to its proximity to the
Pole, than the far north-west. Northern Ungava, though it is no
farther north than Great Slave Lake, is a truly arctic country. But
though the delta of the Mackenzie is more than a thousand miles
to the north-west of Great Slave Lake, trees grow all the way down
the river because Pacific airs reach the Mackenzie Valley and some
Pacific water enters the Beaufort Sea through the Bering Strait.

Arctic experts tell me that the Belcher Islands in Hudson Bay, though they are scarcely farther north than Edinburgh, are as truly "arctic looking" as Ellesmere. A Pole I met on the Slave assured me that the country in that region is pure Siberian. This he well knew, for he had escaped from a concentration camp on the Yenisei.

In no respect do Russia and Canada seem more akin than in the appearance of their great rivers. I have never been in Siberia, and I suppose I should thank God that I haven't, but judging from photographs and from the accounts of people who have been there, I think it safe to say that the great rivers of eastern Russia, despite their immense lengths, are remarkably similar to the Yukon, the Slave, the Mackenzie, the Peace, the Churchill and the Nelson. The Volga and the Don, flowing through the Russian wheat-lands, have the movement and colour of the Saskatchewan, the Moskva wiggles through the Russian capital just as the Red wiggles through Winnipeg, and the Dnieper in places reminds one of parts of the St. Lawrence. However, there is no river in Russia, and to the best of my knowledge none in the world, which resembles the Fraser.

The chief point I am seeking to establish here is that the principal rivers of Canada are northern in nearly all of their general aspects. The glaciers have affected the terrains of nearly all of them, with the result that some of the largest flow through country almost devoid of habitation. The most common trees along their banks are spruce, pine, birch, and – in the west – cottonwood, and the viridian of evergreen forests, splashed here and there by the white trunks of northern birch, gives a sense of vastness, of solitude, of melancholy utterly unlike the lushness of the lower Mississippi or the wildflower and grassy loveliness of the English Thames. The only real lushness I ever found on a Canadian river is in the Thousand Islands section of the St. Lawrence, where the stream sucks through the maze of the archipelago and in summer the air is hot, humid and after dark as influential on the young as flutes and fireflies under the moon. Even in the little province of Nova Scotia, too small to contain a river longer than fifty miles, the trout streams have the clean austerity of burns in the Scottish Highlands.

One of the first things I learned from a study of Canadian rivers is the pointlessness of the old quiz-show gambit, "What is the longest river in the world?" In my own quiz-show days we used to be asked this question once a year, and if I remember correctly, the answers varied. Sometimes it was right to say the Nile, sometimes the Yangtse, sometimes the Ob-Irtish and usually you could get by with the Mississippi-Missouri. The last of these answers gave the whole thing away. This practice of combining the Missouri with the Mississippi in order to give the United States the world's longest river in addition to the world's highest building merely sharpens the absurdity of the old school-book approach to fluvial geography.

Why, I wonder, did they stop with the Missouri? Why not the Mississippi-Missouri-Ohio-Arkansas-Yazoo-Red and several dozen more of the tributaries? No river like the Mississippi can be a simple thing, for it is a united system draining a third of a continent. A river's "greatness" cannot be measured by its length but by the area of its drainage basin, and above all by the accumulation of water which it carries off. In this latter sense every river in the world is minor compared to the two jungle systems, the Congo and the Amazon. Since the bore of the Amazon is visible hundreds of miles out in the sea, anyone particular about measuring this river's "length" should begin with a spring in the Peruvian Andes (if he can be sure of finding the right one) and end at a variable point in the Atlantic between South America and Africa. Any "great" river, to repeat, is a system of waters draining a basin.

If none of the Canadian systems is remarkable for the length of its main stem, this is because of a series of accidents of geography. The north-south continental divide lies in the United States just below the Canadian border. This means that all the important Canadian rivers except the Columbia and the Fraser trend toward the north. Even the St. John runs north for a while before it bends to the east and descends to the Bay of Fundy. Owing to the huge indentations in the northern and eastern coasts of Canada, most of the rivers find their terminus in some body of water not far distant, in global terms, from their sources. The vast, briny tongue of Hudson Bay, extending far south into the Canadian heartland and serving as a funnel to convey polar airs into southern latitudes, catches the Churchill (nearly all of which flows through a grim wilderness) after a run of a thousand miles. The St. Lawrence, pouring easterly and then north-easterly through its trench on the edge of the Laurentian Shield, has not many hundreds of miles to go before it encounters the salt water thrusting into the estuary from the gulf. The Saskatchewan has enough water to flow on and on like the Nile, but less than a thousand miles from its Rocky Mountain source it strikes Lake Winnipeg.

Yet — and this was a matter of great consequence to the nation — Canada contains more inland fresh water than any other country in the world. Apart from the four Great Lakes which she shares with the United States and the large shallow ones of Manitoba (Lake Winnipeg's area is greater than Lake Erie's) there are thousands — probably hundreds of thousands — of small lakes in the Shield and the Northwest Territories. These, of course, are glacial legacies. The river systems of Canada, properly speaking, only in rare instances can be said to include these lakes, but the voyageurs used the lakes as inter-connecting links which enabled them to take their canoes from one river system to another across the country. Incredible though it sounds, the canoe parties which used to leave Montreal in the late eighteenth century were able to paddle nearly all the way to the Pacific coast. Their portages were many and exhausting, yet few of them were longer than three miles. So it came about, thanks to the maze of lakes in the Shield, that Canadian waters could be used as an east-west lateral avenue from the St. Lawrence to the Pacific *above* the American border. That is why it is accurate to say that without the rivers, the early nation could never have survived. The plains and British Columbia would have been fatally severed from the older communities of the Canadian east.

In the Maritime Provinces the only river which properly can be called a system is the St. John, and as river systems go, this is a very small one. The great system of the Canadian east is of course the St. Lawrence. That of the central plains must be called the twin Saskatchewans, for the Churchill flows too far north to matter much to settlement or to the development of the country. The second longest river rising in Canada is the Yukon, but most of it flows through Alaska before, after a weirdly erratic course, it reaches the Bering Sea. In the Rockies the two chief systems are the Fraser and the Columbia, and the far north-west is drained by the largest system of them all, the Mackenzie. In the prairies, however, and in the south-western regions of the Laurentian Shield, there survive remnants of what once was probably the vastest inland freshwater complex in the history of the world, of which the old glacial Lake Agassiz was the heart. But more of this when we come to the Red River.

This brings me to a question which has fascinated me over the past few years, a question which I suppose is really metaphysical. What is a river, anyway? According to the Encyclopedia Britannica, a river is any natural stream of fresh water, larger than a brook or a creek, which flows in a well defined channel. As such, it is a basic geological agent. But though the river carves the channel, its water is always changing – the reason why Heraclitus used a river to illustrate his definition of reality, "Everything Flows." Nobody, as he truly pointed out, can bathe in the same river twice.

This old idea re-occurred to me many times when I contemplated the Columbia Icefield. Out of this massive survival of the Ice Age flow two of the major streams of Canada: the North Saskatchewan and the Athabaska (which merges into the Mackenzie system). Because the Icefield straddles the Great Divide, this makes it possible for the ice to feed rivers which flow, theoretically, into three different oceans. Thus we are told that rivulets leave their source in the Icefield and carry the water to the Pacific, that the Athabaska water reaches the Arctic Ocean by way of the Mackenzie and that the Saskatchewan (since Lake Winnipeg drains into Hudson Bay through the Nelson system) carries some of the Icefield, converted into water, as far as the Atlantic.

But do all these things happen in just this way? Do these little trickles of melt one sees seeping out of the ice really travel all the way to those distant oceans, or are they absorbed into the atmosphere?

Incredibly, we must presume that some of the water from the Icefield really does go all the way down to the various oceans. For consider the Nile which floods regularly, and carries its melted snows far north through the hottest and most arid desert in the world, yet still has an abundance of water to discharge into the Mediterranean. Yet it is certain that a vast weight of Nile water evaporates, and so must a great deal of the water in these northern streams. So once again, what is a river?

The water which evaporates, of course, turns into clouds, and the clouds into rain and snow which may fall as the winds carry them and rejoin other streams quite different from their originals. When Shelley wrote *The Cloud* was he not in a sense also writing of rivers? Is it fanciful to imagine that all the rivers of the northern hemisphere, if not of the world, are in this sense interconnected?

The Rivers that made a Nation

FORT WILLIAM

GRAND
PORTAGE

SAULT-STE-MARIE

GREAT LAKES

GEORGIAN
BAY

MATTAWA
L. NIPPISING

Ottawa
R.

MONTREAL

THREE RIVERS

QUEBEC

St. Lawrence R.

St. John R.

HALIFAX

BOSTON

NEW YORK

The Rivers that made a Nation

If any modern Canadian is curious to know how his country was valued two centuries ago, all he need do is recall some of the sentiments it inspired among famous men at that time. Voltaire's dismissal of the St. Lawrence Valley as "a few acres of snow" is almost too well known to repeat; it is less well known that Montcalm, who now is a Canadian hero, loathed the country he fought to defend. The British never valued Canada for herself. Just before the peace conference which ended the Seven Years War there was strong pressure in England in favour of trading Canada back to France in return for Guadeloupe. This little Carib isle grew sugar which makes rum, and because many people like rum, rum will always have an economic future.

But in early days few people liked the Land of Cain or the Land of Snows, nor did many believe that it could possibly have an economic future worth mentioning. Had it not been for the strategic necessity of securing the St. Lawrence as a high-road into the Ohio Territory, and also of protecting the northern flank of the rich Thirteen Colonies, Guadeloupe might easily have been England's choice.

Nor would the British of that time have been absurd if they had made such a choice. Canada may have had, as Dr. Johnson remarked of Lapland and the Scottish Highlands, "prodigious wild and noble prospects", but the Age of Reason saw nothing beautiful in wild and noble prospects, and certainly nothing useful. Least of all could the British recognize any economic future in a terrain shaggy with evergreens and horrid (to them the word meant "bristling") with the rocky outcroppings of the Pre-Cambrian Shield. In addition to all these disadvantages there was the Canadian climate.

Once more we cannot consider the British to have been stupid. The gold and practical metals of the Shield were still locked there, hidden, awaiting a twentieth-century technology to make them available to men. Two centuries ago nobody understood the value of petroleum, least of all did they know that a lake of it existed under the Alberta plain. From the servants of the Hudson's Bay Company the English might have picked up some vague information about prairie soils, but they would have presumed them unfavourable to any large creatures except the buffalo which browsed and multiplied in the knee-high grass of a pasture a thousand miles wide. After fearful hardships the Selkirk settlers managed to keep themselves alive in Manitoba, but for decades they were the most isolated farmers in North America. Railways had to be built, farm implements mechanized, grain elevators invented before wheat growing could become the huge industry it is today. As for the timber of the Canadian east, it never transcended a local use before Napoleon sealed off the Baltic ports from British shipping and made it profitable for Canadian business men to export timber for the masts and decks of the Royal Navy. Most of Canada, just like Siberia, had to wait for the age of technology before it could be developed.

Two centuries ago – and this the English understood when they toyed with the idea of exchanging Canada for Guadeloupe – the sole profitable Canadian enterprises were fur trading and the coastal fisheries. Of these, only the former was of real and continuing interest to the capitals of Europe.

Far different was the situation south of what is now the Canadian-American border. With climates ranging from temperate to sub-tropical, the American English soon developed an economy of considerable variety. Towns and cities flourished on the fertile lands between the sea and the Appalachians. The ports were all ice-free and in easy contact with Europe and the West Indies. By the middle of the eighteenth century a mature urban culture had grown in cities like Boston, New York, Philadelphia, Baltimore and Charleston, and its capacity to offer outlets to a variety of human resources and talents was soon proved by the kind of men it produced. The careers, interests and abilities of men like Benjamin Franklin, Thomas Jefferson and John Jay were of a kind that could not have been developed in the Canada of that time, any more than the careers and abilities of men like Peter Pond and Alexander Mackenzie could have been developed within the Thirteen Colonies. Sophistication is the product of universities and the variety of urban life, epic adventures of a society much more primitive.

In the early days the Canadian experience was epic, and the price of such an experience is roughness and lack of education. As late as 1800, James McGill wrote to the Governor of Lower Canada that not one boy in five in the Montreal area could write his own name. Reading and writing was of no use to a canoe man, (nearly all the *engagés* in the fur trade signed with an X) and for a hundred and fifty years young French Canadians had been growing up along the St. Lawrence expecting to earn their livings on the rivers leading into the west.

For this reason alone, urban growth in Canada was extremely slow, and the seniority of a few Canadian cities is no indication whatever of a cultural maturity. Though Quebec was founded some dozen years before the landing of the Pilgrims in Massachusetts, and in the mid-eighteenth century had an imposing presence on its rock above the river, it was really more fortress than city. Louisbourg in Cape Breton Island was rightly named the Gibraltar of America: nearly all of its citizens were soldiers. Halifax, founded in 1749, was originally intended as a naval and military base and only developed into a true city after the American Revolution. As for Montreal, up to the end of the Napoleonic Wars, when its population was verging on 20,000, it could almost be described as a supply depot and base camp for the fur trade carried on in the interior.

But early Canada possessed one asset the Americans lacked: the St. Lawrence River. Its rapids halted sailing ships just above Montreal, but the river struck directly through the gap between the Laurentian and Appalachian chains, and the French Canadians used it. While the Americans remained penned between the mountains and the sea, it was the high honour of the French Canadians that their boldest spirits sallied out from the St. Lawrence to explore and map nearly all of the continental interior which Americans and English-speaking Canadians now occupy. Many Americans today believe that their own West was unknown before the mountain men went up the Missouri, but French-Canadian voyageurs had been there long before the mountain men. When Francis Parkman went out on the Oregon Trail in 1846, the epic period of French-Scottish-Canadian exploration was over. But the reliable guides Parkman found in the Missouri country were all French Canadians. They were the last in a long chain of frontier adventurers whose abilities had been developed by the fur trade.

By its very nature this was a river trade. The rivers brought the traders and the Indians into contact with each other, and from the beginning the French had a wonderful naturalness in getting on with the Indians. The tributaries and backwaters of the great river systems were breeding grounds for the animals, and most of the valuable fur-bearing animals are amphibious. In early times the beaver was the animal whose fur was most highly valued in Europe, and for a curious reason: it served as raw material for the hat trade in a period when the wearing of costly hats was deemed essential to a man's status as a fine gentleman. By another of history's ironies — and Canadian history has been a huge congeries of ironies — this wild and dangerous trade owed its support to a temporary fashion in the capitals of Europe.

The dominance of the fur trade conspired with conditions of soil and climate to retard the development of a true Canadian culture. Not only was fur trading a nomadic occupation; it discouraged settlement everywhere because settlement drove off the animals. It could never afford to employ a large body of workers in the field, and the great majority of these were ignorant men who regarded themselves as a class apart, very much like mercenary soldiers in the old days. Since some of the leaders — Alexander Mackenzie, for instance, David Thompson, Alexander Henry and William McGillivray — had intelligence and sensitivity, they hated the harshness and semi-savagery of life in the field, though the goal that urged them onward never failed to give them a mental and moral dominance over the men they led.

Even the habits of the beaver tribe conspired to turn the early Canadians into rovers who departed further and further from civilization. The beaver is not a remarkably prolific animal: if let alone, the beaver population never increases by more than 20% annually. When the Europeans first arrived in America there were, according to later computations, about ten million beaver on the continent, their numbers varying between ten to fifty per square mile in the regions where they bred. This was not a large number considering the destructiveness of the trade. The beaver's habits made it impossible for him to escape his enemies because he was not a migrant. He lived in lodges. As David Thompson noted, the beaver "could be attacked at any convenient time and in all seasons, and thus their numbers were reduced."

They were reduced so rapidly that in the Maritime Provinces the fur trade was virtually dead after a few years of European depredation. As early as 1635, only twenty-seven years after the founding of Quebec, beaver had almost vanished in the region about Three Rivers, despite the fact that the St. Maurice is a great tributary which still, for most of its course, flows through uninhabited land. Champlain himself recognized that if he hoped to retain the interest of his home government in the colony of New France, the fur trade would have to be carried into the interior. *His* primary interest may have been to find the Northwest Passage to the Sea of Japan, but he was practical enough to see that if this venture was to be financed, it would have to be paid for in beaver.

It was Champlain who was the first European to recognize that if Canadians were to move in a forested country they would have to forget about horses and even about European methods of navigation. Cartier had been stopped at Lachine, and so was he:

"The water here is so swift that it could not be more so . . . so that it is impossible to imagine one's being able to go by boats through these falls. But anyone desiring to pass them, should provide himself with the canoe of the savages, which a man can easily carry."

So began, with Champlain's first tentative journey in a crazy birch-bark canoe above Montreal, the first chapter in the long saga of voyaging. The canoe, as has sometimes been suggested, would make as accurate a symbol on our coat of arms as the beaver, and the birch tree a truer emblem than the maple. Canada is one of the few countries which did not depend for its early development on the horse. In the Canadian bush a horse could neither eat nor move; if you merely tethered him there the mosquitoes and blackflies would kill him or drive him mad. But the birch-bark canoe could go wherever there was a foot of water to float it, and was so light that even the largest could be carried by a few men. The canoe made possible the careers of generation after generation of explorers who were to follow the rivers of America from Montreal to the Gulf of Mexico, to the Beaufort Sea, and finally to the Pacific Ocean.

It was Champlain, as Bartlet Brebner suggests, who invented the strange trade of voyageur, with its even stranger derivative, the *coureur de bois*. The difference between them was technically a legal one. The *coureur de bois* was an individualist who operated without a licence, and when he first appeared in the west, the servants of the Hudson's Bay Company called him a pedlar. But voyaging, as it was conceived by some of the greater spirits who engaged in it, was more than fur trading. Though men like Radisson, LaSalle, LaVérendrye, Samuel Hearne, Alexander Mackenzie, David Thompson and Simon Fraser were certainly in the fur-trading business, essentially they were explorers.

Once Champlain had begun the fur trade along the interior waterways, the voyages multiplied with a rapidity which still astonishes the historian. So mobile was the canoe, so enticing the next bend around the river, so dominant the human instinct to know what lay around it, that within the course of a very few years the voyageurs of French Canada were in the heartland of the continent. The names of some of them ring like bugle calls in the North American story — some of them the greatest in continental history before the age of Washington.

Etienne Brûlé, one of Champlain's "young men", almost certainly reached the Chaudière Falls on the Ottawa as early as 1610. Two years afterwards he became the first European to reach the Sweetwater Sea, as Lake Huron was then called.

Radisson, with his brother-in-law Groseilliers, was probably west of Lake Michigan by the mid-1650s. During this period (the dates are uncertain) the pair entered Lake Superior and *discovered a portage over which other unknown voyageurs, possibly French, had passed before them!* Soon after this they were in Minnesota at the top of the drainage basin of the greatest river on the continent. When the government of New France, which seldom had the quality of its greatest subjects, confiscated the furs of Radisson and Groseilliers on the excuse that they lacked a licence to trade, they went over to the English, and one result of their doing so was the founding of the Hudson's Bay Company.

The two priests, Marquette and Jolliet, descended the Mississippi as far as the Arkansas in 1673, and thereby established beyond doubt the existence of a practicable water avenue from the St. Lawrence to the Gulf of Mexico.

They were followed a decade later by Cavelier de la Salle. In 1680, LaSalle was on the upper Mississippi with Père Hennepin, and in 1682 he reached the delta of the river and claimed the region later known as the Louisiana Territory for the French king.

About two decades later Sieur de Bienville, who may have been born in Montreal, became the first official governor of Louisiana. A road had been found and developed, though it was very thinly held, from Quebec City to the Gulf of Mexico. The French, using the rivers as only they knew how, had drawn a vast loop about the English colonists who still were confined to the Atlantic seaboard.

The last of the supremely great French discoverers, and surely one of the most interesting, was Pierre Gaultier de Varennes, Sieur de la Vérendrye. Born in Three Rivers in 1685 (the same year, incidentally, in which Handel and Johann Sebastian Bach were born) LaVérendrye first served in colonial wars, then went to Europe to fight in the War of the Spanish Succession. After his final return to Canada, a man over forty, he took to the rivers. Armed with a monopoly for the far western fur trade, LaVérendrye was at Grand Portage in 1731 with a party of fifty including three of his sons. He worked out a successful route through the maze of small streams, lakes and muskeg of the western Shield, and in 1734 the first white man's fort stood on the black earth of Manitoba. The vast central plain lay open to him. The Assiniboine and the South Saskatchewan wound across it and led men of the LaVérendrye party to a sight of mountains, possibly the Rockies, a little more than one hundred and thirty years after Brûlé reached the Chaudière Falls.

Nothing in later years was as epic as the sustained efforts of these early Frenchmen. It could not be. In later years the white men were better armed, and though the Indians in the Canadian west could be dangerous, they seldom if ever displayed the appalling cruelty and military vigour of the eastern savages who tortured Brébeuf to death. After the Hurons killed Etienne Brûlé, they ate him.

These facts are familiar: I repeat them only to underline the desperate nature of the early Canadian experience. There was no discharge from this war, at least not for the dedicated man. The isolation of the voyageurs, the knowledge that they were self-condemned to a life of hardship and danger before which, ultimately, their physical and moral powers were bound to fail — these thoughts haunted the bravest and boldest among them. They lacked the consolation of soldiers who risk their lives, for what they did was done without an audience, without the support of a disciplined regiment or army. They could not even communicate their experiences to civilized men, because civilized men lacked the knowledge and background to understand what they meant when they told them that the winter had descended before they could reach a base camp, or that such and such a number of portages had been made or rapids run in such and such a number of days.

Thoughts like these were in Radisson's mind when he wrote a passage with the force of poetry:

"What fairer bastion than a good tongue, especially when one sees his owne chimney smoak, or when we can kisse our owne wife or kisse our neighbour's wife with ease and delight? It is a different thing when victuals are wanting, worke whole nights & dayes, lye down on the bare ground, & not always that hap, the breech in the water, the feare in the buttocks, to have the belly empty, the wearinesse in the bones, the drowsinesse in the body by the bad weather you are to suffer, having nothing to keep you from such calamity."

When New France fell and was ceded to England in 1763, the control of the Canadian fur trade passed from the French forever. English-speaking men, most of them Scottish Highlanders, now appear in the trade working with the experienced French-Canadian voyageurs who served under them in the North West Company as *engagés*. It was a partnership vital for the future of Canada, and the beginning of the Scottish influence in Canadian affairs.

For it was about this time that the Highland Scotch had finally reached the end of their long, brave but self-damaging struggle for independence against the Anglo-Saxons of the south. The English had conquered them in 1745 and doomed the clansman's way of life. At the best of times it had been a poor life in a poor country: it has been remarked more than once that only the Highlanders and the French Canadians had the necessary background of poverty to qualify them for work on the Canadian rivers. Already the Hudson's Bay Company, scouring the British Isles for men hardy, desperate and disciplined enough to entice into the trade, had been recruiting Orkneymen from the rocks of Ultima Thule, shipping them by the northern route into Hudson Bay and putting them to work there.

Simon McTavish, the master of the North West Company, lived in Montreal like a lord and had something of the temperament and style of a Highland chief of the better sort, though his Scottish ancestry was probably less exalted than he liked to pretend. All of these Highlanders — as distinct from the patient Orkneymen

— had the intense personal pride of a race never noted for its emotional balance. This may have been one reason why they had so little sympathy for the slogans of the democratic revolution then brewing in the Thirteen Colonies. That revolution came out of the middle classes, and the Highlands had never had a middle class.

The fire, the imagination and the boldness of these Highland leaders transformed the whole character of the fur trade and turned it into an enterprise in which business considerations, at least as seen by a cool-headed man, very often took a second place to dreams. When the American Revolution broke out, James McGill (a Glasgow man originally) instantly recognized that if the Americans won the war the south-west of the continent would soon be closed to the Canadian fur trade. When he realized that the Americans were on the point of victory, he sold his shares in the company. But Simon McTavish met the challenge by pushing it right over the edge of the map. He bet his fortune on the Athabaska region. The tenacity of McTavish and his colleagues in the face of appalling obstacles can almost be called sublime. Under the best of circumstances, fur trading was a gamble in which the margin of profit over cost was never very great. Though 'a few large fortunes were made in it, they were acquired by penny-pinching and a driving of the *engagés* to a degree which would horrify a modern labour union. But McTavish and his associates did not hesitate. Not even the complete success of the American Revolution lessened their compulsion to expand. Ironically, it was the blind obstinacy of these Highlanders which limited the plans of some of the shrewdest American statesmen who ever lived.

When Benjamin Franklin, John Adams and John Jay met the English diplomats in Versailles in 1783 to draft the treaty which ended the Revolutionary War, one of their chief objects was to destroy permanently the British ability to threaten the new Republic. The British were still entrenched in Nova Scotia and the St. Lawrence; the Americans had not yet moved out in any large degree beyond the Appalachians. The question of the boundary between the United States and what remained of British North America was therefore the most vital question at this conference.

The boundary to which the British finally agreed was a triumph for the United States and a permanent disaster for Canada. The British were so ignorant of North American geography they did not understand what they were giving away, and they had invited no Canadians to the conference who might have told them. Ever since 1783, the Canadian population has been penned between the Shield and the border in narrow strips. The St. Lawrence and the four northern Great Lakes were split down the middle between the two countries. Montreal was cut off totally from the Ohio Territory and the Mississippi Valley, and as a final touch, Grand Portage was slipped in just underneath the new border so that it reposed in the United States. However, the British did insist on gaining equal rights along the Pigeon and Rainy rivers, and this was to be of vital importance to Canada. It left open a canoe route to the prairies and the far west.

The Montreal fur-traders had few illusions about what this border would mean to them. In time, and the time would not be long, they would be forbidden to do any business at all in the wilderness south of the border which Canadians had explored and opened up to trade. Even Grand Portage would be closed to them. So the North West Company moved their inland base to a new site at Fort William. The cost of doing so came to £10,000.

From this time until the North West Company was absorbed by the Bay in 1821, the Montreal traders met one of the most remarkable challenges in the history of commerce. As they depended on the far north-west for their furs, they were now committed to an operation in which the supply lines were stretched to a limit which would make any normal, hard-headed man of commerce turn pale. The pelts had to be paid for in trade goods conveyed three-quarters of the way across the continent in birch-bark canoes. The pay loads had to be paddled and portaged back to Montreal over a distance of some three thousand miles. The market, nearly all of it in Europe, was still another three thousand miles to the east across the Atlantic Ocean.

Speed and efficiency of the highest kind, supported by an *esprit de corps* among the canoemen as intense as that of a championship hockey team, were the sole possible replies to a challenge so stern. The travel schedules set for the voyageurs seem incredible to the modern imagination.

Leaving Lachine in "brigades" of three to four canoes, with an experienced guide in the leading craft, the voyageurs from Montreal first set out for the Grand River, as the Ottawa was then called. At Sainte-Anne-de-Bellevue they always stopped to pray in the chapel to the saint who protects travellers on water, and this rite gave rise to Thomas Moore's famous poem:

Faintly as tolls the evening chime
Our voices keep tune and our oars keep time,
Soon as the woods on the shore look dim
We'll sing at St. Ann's our parting hymn,
Row, brothers, row! The stream runs fast,
The rapids are near and the daylight's past . . .

This poem, written in soft music by a cultivated visitor to Canada, using the word "oars" instead of "paddles", depreciates its subject. The Homer of the *Iliad* might have risen to the experience of the voyageurs, but not the sweet poet of Ireland.

After paddling and portaging the Ottawa as far as Mattawa, the canoes turned south toward Lake Nipissing, crossed it, and descended the French River into Georgian Bay. Then they paddled west along the North Channel above Manitoulin Island, working in the dead or choppy waters of the lake and often losing several days if the winds were contrary. They called the wind *la vieille* (the old woman), and if she was behind them they could raise a sail. But if she was heavy against them — and the prevailing winds in the region are contrary to west-bound canoes — they often had to put up on the shore because the high, steep waves of the inland lakes would break the backs of their canoes. When they went to Michilimackinac they were expected to reach their destination within a period of from thirty-five to forty days, and the same time was expected when they were bound for Grand Portage and Fort William. This voyage was accomplished with canoes fully loaded with trade goods, and there were thirty-six portages between Lachine and the Lakehead, some of them longer than a "league". In the voyageur's language, a "league" was roughly two miles. If express canoes without cargo were used, as they sometimes were on special occasions, the time was much faster. A letter survives dated in Montreal on May 6, 1817, which was received at Rainy Lake beyond Fort William on June 3.

What these voyages involved in hardship, labour and moral stamina can no more be revealed by the historian's method of stating the facts than the truth of a battle can be conveyed by the communiqué issued by the high command after the fighting is over and the dead have been counted. From Julius Caesar to the P.R.s of the Pentagon, the truth of life and death has always been hidden behind facts and statistics. That is the trouble with history.

It is probably an unavoidable trouble, but it certainly explains why so few people learn much from it.

"Our men moved their camp, marched twenty miles, and at night they placed their camp in a suitable place" — how many of us welcomed lines like these when we studied the *Gallic War* in school! They occurred so often we did not have to pause to work out the grammar. But they told us nothing of the realities.

On every step of that twenty-mile march, probably through hostile country, the legionaries had to carry their weapons and food, their armour and personal necessities, a total weight close to a hundred pounds per man. When the "suitable place" was reached, it was usually on a hill with a forest nearby. While one detachment marked out the lines of the camp, another dug a trench about it and still another went into the woods to cut trees. After the trunks had been trimmed, sawn up and sharpened at one end, they were dragged to the suitable place and staked into the ground just behind the lip of the trench. Only after all this work was done could the soldier wrap himself in his cloak and fall asleep on the ground.

A similar recovery of reality is essential if any modern man is to understand the truth about life on the Canadian rivers in the voyaging days.

On May 25, 1793, a young Scot called John Macdonell set out from Lachine on his first voyage with a brigade of the North West Company. He has left a diary of that voyage written in the usual terse language of the communiqué, and he has also recorded, with the distances distinctly stated, the nature of each of the thirty-six portages between Montreal and Grand Portage — here the carrying place was nine miles long — as well as the character of the streams and lakes. With the help of the imagination, the record is a fascinating one, the more so because this was a routine voyage.

On this stage of the journey into the west, the larger canoes carried loads varying from three to four tons and were manned by crews of eight or ten men. The middle men, using short paddles, sat two abreast while the bowman and steersman were placed higher and were equipped with paddles much longer. The Montreal canoe was thirty-five to forty feet long made entirely of the bark of yellow birch placed over ribs of thin white cedar with thwarts numbering between four and nine and boards four inches wide secured just below the gunwales as seats for the paddlemen.

The bark was secured by melted pine gum, and after a heavy rapid or a day's paddling the seams had to be re-gummed to prevent leaking. The canoe used by Alexander Mackenzie, and specially designed for his exploration of the Rockies, was so light that it could be carried by two men. But the weight of a large canoe out of Montreal was much greater than this, and required at least four men on the portage. The whole operation of portaging brings up an interesting calculation in the mathematics of labour, sweat and tired muscles.

Superlatives have bothered me all through the writing of this book, but I cannot avoid them without diminishing what seems to me the truth. Every new thing I have learned about the Canadian voyageur seems to me more incredible than the last. His deeds originated the Paul Bunyan myths of the American north-west, and Paul Bunyan was an inheritor of Hercules and Mercury in folklore. But the true and proved facts concerning the life of the voyageur are such that I can only say that if I, physically, am a man, he, physically, was a superman.

On portages the load that had to be moved, divided up among the crew, usually totalled more than four hundred pounds per man not counting the canoe. Every man of the crew was expected to carry at least two "pieces" of goods, each weighing ninety pounds, but so great was the emulation among them that some individuals often carried three pieces or even four. They did not walk with these loads: *they carried them at a dog trot* bent half-double with the pieces on their backs and secured there by a leather band, called a tumpline, which was passed around their foreheads. More than one traveller conveyed by voyageurs in the canoes has testified that without any load at all he could barely move as fast as these men did with two hundred pounds on their backs. Finally, because they worked at the height of the insect season, the voyageurs were encased over the carrying places in humming, stinging envelopes of mosquitoes and blackflies.

In addition to the portaging there was the tracking of canoes against heavy currents and the running of rapids. The rapids were always risky, and crosses marked the graves of drowned voyageurs on the banks, clusters of them all the way from the Long Sault on the Ottawa to the mouth of the Winnipeg River. Tracking could be a nightmare. The men had to get out and haul by ropes attached to bow and stern (two ropes were essential to prevent the canoe from yawing in against the shore) and this meant slithering over wet rocks slimy with vegetable growth, stumbling over the usual litter of fallen trees and sometimes wading breast high in the stream. As I know from personal experience, the silt along the banks of the Assiniboine, Saskatchewan and Mackenzie is deep and soft, and after rain it has the consistency of porridge and sometimes the texture of axle grease. Along the Fraser when the men had to do a great deal of tracking under appalling difficulties, they wore out a pair of moccasins a day and had to make themselves new ones. While tracking canoes, the men were more plagued by insects even than when they portaged, because there were usually more of them along the water's edge. So paddling in a free river or in an open lake came as a marvellous release, and when the men swung into the stroke they broke into song. That was when time was made up. The mileage from Montreal to Georgian Bay was little more than the mileage from the mouth of French River through the Sault to the head of Lake Superior, and here the figures of John Macdonell tell their own story. It took his brigade thirty-one days to reach Lake Huron from Sainte-Anne. But though they lost a day through a storm on the lake, they reached Grand Portage from French River in just under ten days! Look at the map, remember that most of the time they were travelling against the wind, and try to believe that this was merely a routine voyage!

At Grand Portage or Fort William the Montreal men ended their runs. The Company's agent met the wintering partners from the north-west, and the trade goods were forwarded over the height of land by a special body of men to the Company's fort on Rainy Lake, the eastern terminus of *les vrais hommes du nord* who had come down across the plains from the Athabaska country. At Grand Portage or Fort William the Montreal crews had a brief time for carousing and eating, then they re-loaded their canoes with the furs and set out on the return trail to Montreal with the pay loads. If they did not get back before winter, they were frozen in and had to survive as best they could. A failure to return in time also meant a disastrous financial loss to the Company.

At Rainy Lake the true Northmen took over, and these were the élite of the service. They paddled through Lake of the Woods and by a series of smaller lakes and interconnecting streams (the Winnipeg River was exhaustingly cursed by rapids) into Lake Winnipeg itself. In earlier times canoe parties used to paddle from there up the Red River into Minnesota toward the sources of the

Mississippi, but after the American Revolution the goal was the north-western edge of the North American map, Lake Athabaska and the Peace River country. The Saskatchewan and Athabaskan brigades paddled north up Lake Winnipeg to the mouth of the Saskatchewan River and then — after some very severe portages — they worked up against the current of the North Branch to Cumberland Lake and thence to Frog Portage, which made a bridge to the Churchill River. This powerful stream, against which they also had to paddle, led them to the Methye Portage (or Portage LaLoche), a very tough one with a sharp height of land at the end of it. The Methye took them to the Clearwater, a tributary of the Athabaska, and then they coasted down that great river of the north-west into Lake Athabaska and reached their chief north-western base at Fort Chipewyan. In the later years of the North West Company the brigades went even beyond this. They paddled up to Fort Vermilion on the Peace, and later still the fur-traders established themselves in forts on the Fraser and the Columbia.

This final leap across two-fifths of Ontario, across Manitoba, Saskatchewan and some or all of Alberta, all of it trending north, was a race against time even more intense than the run from Montreal to the head of Lake Superior. So close was the margin between the meeting with the Montreal canoes and the coming of frost that a delay of a few days might ruin a whole voyage. According to Alexander Mackenzie, the Athabaskan brigades generally left Rainy Lake on the first of August, and had to reach Chipewyan inside two months.

What of the canoes and of the men themselves?

By the time the North West Company was established, the art of canoe-handling had so matured on the rivers that the French Canadians were much more mobile than the men of the Hudson's Bay Company. British as they were, the Bay men clung for a long time to wooden *bateaux*. The Nor'westers used two types of canoe which they called the *canot du maître* and the *canot du nord*, the former for the run out of Montreal, the latter, which was lighter and carried less than a ton and a half of cargo, for the run west of Fort William where the streams were shallower and tracking more frequent. The *canot du nord* often carried a crew of no more than five men.

But the *canot du maître* was a considerable craft. It had a wide beam, a remarkably high strake and high, curved bows. It was gaily painted and travelled with a pennant blowing out from its stern and often with the picture of an Indian's head on its bows. A variety of pictures of these larger canoes survive and one of them has a feature which — at least to me — was more interesting than the canoe itself.

This was no less a personage than Sir George Simpson, the "Big Bourgeois" of the Hudson's Bay Company, the chief destroyer of the Nor'westers, and in his old age one of the richest men in Montreal. After the Bay absorbed the North West Company they not only employed the skilled Canadian voyageurs; even before that time they had adopted the classic Canadian canoes. In this picture Simpson sits in the middle wearing a top hat of massive proportions, as did many of the bourgeois (this was the old French name for the proprietor or company partner) while *en voyage*. The top hat was a mark of their quality and station. In Simpson's canoe the paddlemen are seated as usual two abreast and the bowman and steersman are in their usual places. But directly behind Simpson, who wears a grim expression on one of the most haughty faces in Canadian history, are a pair of undersized, wild-looking characters blowing bagpipes.

The presence of these pipers in Simpson's canoe gives the Big Bourgeois an extra dimension. People who worked for him knew that he was the toughest employer there ever was in a notoriously tough trade. He pinched pennies, he was ruthless, he squeezed out of his servants the last ounce of work, he paid them as little as he possibly could. One knows that Simpson understood the value of every square foot of every canoe or York boat in the service of his company. And yet, there sits that pair of private pipers! The Scotch are a peculiar people, and never more so than when they try to out-English the English in cold calculation after they have gone into business and made a success of it. But the old wildness never quite leaves the pure Scot. Behind the granite features of George Simpson, underneath his brutal surface callousness, the primitive heat burned, and hence that pair of pipers. Without them, the *canot du maître* could have carried at least two hundred more pounds of trade goods. Yet Simpson sacrificed money for the pipers, and I like to think of him sitting there in his stove-pipe hat, the mosquitoes buzzing in his hair, the canoe swaying down a rapid through the forest wilderness, and that pair of wee pipers behind him blowing his ears off.

But there were no pipers, no luxuries, for the average *engagé* — the paid voyageur of the fur-trading companies. Day after day from dawn to dusk, sometimes for eighteen hours daily, they drove those loaded canoes back and forth across the continent. As they paddled they sang the old French songs and some others of their own making. In favouring currents they could swing the stroke easily, but in adverse currents or dead water their paddles bit hard. The average rate of stroking was forty to the minute, but often they stroked at the rate of one per second, in perfect time and with only a few stops in the course of the day. The stops were called "a pipe", and their length depended on the state of the men. Travellers carried in canoes have testified that after twelve hours' paddling, with only three rests of ten to fifteen minutes each, those incredible French Canadians refused to stop because they were still "fresh". Their sense of competition with one another was Homeric. Duncan McGillivray once witnessed a race in Lake Winnipeg between Athabaska men and a rival brigade. The men paddled all out *for forty-eight consecutive hours without once leaving their canoes!* A steersman collapsed into sleep, fell overboard and would have been drowned had not his own canoe gone back to pick him up; he was sinking under the weight of his clothes and in a state of shock from the frigid water. In this race as the men stroked, the guides cut off hunks of pemmican and thrust them into the mouths of the paddlers.

What manner of men were these — giants? Actually, they were built more like gnomes. In 1826 an American, Thomas L. McKenney, visited the trading routes of Canada and described the voyageurs as follows:

"They are short, thick set, and active, and never tire. A Canadian, if born to be a labourer, deems himself to be very unfortunate if he should chance to grow over five feet five, or six inches — and if he shall reach five feet ten or eleven, it forever excludes him from the privilege of becoming voyageur. There is no room for the legs of such people, in these canoes. But if he shall stop growing at about five feet four inches, and be gifted with a good voice, and lungs that never tire, he is considered as having been born under a most favourable star."

Freedom, T. E. Lawrence once wrote, is man's second need: here is the sole explanation of those men's willingness to engage in a trade like this, which in time was sure to break them. Though there were many instances of river men keeping on working into late middle-age, the voyageurs as a rule died young. They were lucky if they were not double-ruptured and suffering from spastic backs before they were forty. But at least they were free from the forelock-tugging kind of poverty their class had to endure in Europe. They had the pride of champions which is the surest of all proofs of an inner sense of personal value. Freedom has always been the most expensive possession in the world, and the price for it has been paid in different coin from age to age. In the early days of Canada, the coin was hardship and endurance.

There were rains and cold nights, and the only women of the interior were virtual savages. The food the men ate on the rivers makes the diet of a modern Canadian work camp seem like the fare of a Roman emperor of the decadence. On the eastern run to the Lakehead the voyageurs were called *mangeurs de lard*, or pork-eaters, and the French word gives us a good idea of the quality of the pork. In the west pemmican was the stable diet, and no more nourishing one was ever invented, but even with wild rice added, boiled pemmican at the end of sixteen hours of labour is not much to look forward to. If the schedule was not too exacting, the men fished and hunted and searched for birds' eggs, but if food ran out they would eat anything. Often they literally ate crow. The poor French voyageur, especially in the early days, usually had nothing better to eat than a kind of hominy made of split dried peas or corn impregnated with fat.

But of all the ordeals faced by the river men, that of the winterer was the worst. He was the one who had to stay out in the wilderness perhaps two thousand miles from his base. The Indians brought him furs, and though he often had an Indian wife, he sometimes was entirely alone. If game was abundant he ate well, and there was usually plenty of fish preserved from the fall through the winter. But if game failed or fish rotted, starvation or dysentery was his fate. If he fell sick there was no help for him, and his loneliness was total in a six months' winter when the prairie was nothing but a white death.

Narrow this life was, uncivilized and uneducated, but on the whole it was less brutalizing than the life in the lumber camps in the Victorian era. At the principal bases of the Hudson's Bay Company all the men were required to attend prayers regularly. There is a poignant memorandum dating from the early eighteenth-century records of the Bay which enjoins the Company's servants "to live lovingly with one another not to swear or quarrel but to live peaceably without drunkenness or profaneness." The

Nor'westers had a rougher tradition but more personal independence within the service; less consciousness, perhaps, that they were suffering a thankless exploitation by rich men who never troubled themselves to know at what price of human stamina and hardship the profits were earned. Nearly all the Montreal partners in the Company had served at least some time on the rivers. The French-Canadian voyageur, though not fond of washing *en route*, was a considerable dandy whenever he neared a post. Even though the only women in the post were savages, he washed and put on his best clothes. He had a Gallic courtesy to counteract his almost incredible toughness, and Francis Parkman writes feelingly of the human quality of his *Canadien* guides along the Missouri. As for the Highlanders in the service of the fur trade, one of them wrote the "Lone Shieling" poem, possibly the most haunting verses ever composed in Canada.

The fur trade failed in the end; it was doomed the moment the settlers began moving into the west to farm. Long before that time there were men engaged in it who had seen the writing on the wall. Sometimes when I walk up the avenue of the McGill campus and reach the Founder's tomb, I think back on the life he led and the shrewd Lowland caution which prompted James McGill to take his money out of the fur trade in time. He had never been a true voyageur, merely a poor boy from Scotland who had entered the only Canadian trade which offered him a living. He had earned his place in the Beaver Club by a winter spent alone near the headwaters of the Mississippi, but he got off the rivers before the life on them broke him. McGill lacked the transcendent imagination of Simon McTavish and the last-ditch loyalty of William McGillivray, but he had much common sense. Unlike most of his old colleagues in the fur trade, he did not die broke. His life had taught him that civilization could never grow in Canada under the conditions he had known in his youth. Though he was well off by colonial standards, he would never have been accounted an especially rich man in England. He left just enough to make it possible to found a college. Today McGill University lies like a quiet pattern of order in the roaring tumult of modern Montreal, and is by far the most important visible monument to the North West Company's great adventure.

For the economic contribution of the fur trade after the American Revolution has surely been exaggerated. It is a common argument that furs saved the country from being absorbed by the United States because they provided an east-west trade, all Canadian, in a continent where the normal lines of economic communication run north and south with the greater power and population of the United States sucking the wealth of Canada southward. I cannot believe this. The fur trade may have bridged an economic gap for a number of years, but the true reason why it saved Canada from absorption was not economic. It was political.

Not only did the voyageurs explore most of North America; after 1783 they staked out Canadian — or, at that time, British — claims to the whole north-western hinterland from the head of the Lakes to the Pacific. When the tide of homesteaders fanned out from the railheads in the American mid-west in the nineteenth century, the Canadian west would surely have been occupied by them, and subsequently claimed as American territory by the American government, had not the ancient rights of prior exploration, which the Americans respected, bound the land to Canada. The lonely posts were on the plains, in the Fraser and Columbia valleys, on the Pacific coast, and the Union Jack flew over all of them. Yet only a handful of men achieved this result. At the height of its power the North West Company may have employed as many as five thousand men, but less than two thousand were in service in the field between Montreal and Chipewyan. It was not their numbers that counted, but what they did. And in the long run what was done by the dreamers mattered the most.

David Thompson was probably the greatest geographer ever developed in North America; without his work, backed by Simon Fraser's voyage down the river which bears his name, it is hard to believe that British Columbia would now be a Canadian province. And of course there was Alexander Mackenzie, the prince of all the Canadian explorers.

A dozen years before Lewis and Clark, Mackenzie reached the Pacific through North America. He threaded to the end the Northwest Passage. Its reality bore no resemblance to the European dream of a great gorge which would float sailing ships from the Old World through the continental land mass of the New. It was simply the chain of rivers, lakes and portages which enabled canoes from Montreal to move all the way from the St. Lawrence across Canada to the northern and western oceans.

"Alexander Mackenzie, from Canada, by land, the twenty-second of July, one thousand seven hundred and ninety-three" — this celebrated understatement, scrawled in a mixture of vermilion and grease on a rock in Dean Channel after Mackenzie's passage down the Bella Coola, wrote *finis* to a quest begun exactly three hundred and one years earlier when Christopher Columbus set out across the Atlantic from Palos. The reality found by Mackenzie served only to dissipate the dream. But it introduced a new reality, just as Columbus' lost quest drew an entire hemisphere into the story of civilization. How strange that a Canadian birch-bark canoe without a name, last in a long succession of canoes from Champlain's first one, should have earned a place in the company of ships like the *Santa Maria* and the *Golden Hind*!

Interlude

Forsan et haec olim meminisse iuvabit — no, it does not always follow that in later years it is a pleasure to remember hardship, passion and suffering. In the eighteenth century, when Englishmen for the first time in their history could afford to relax and begin to enjoy life, there was a general and polite forgetting of the heroic age of Elizabeth and the struggle for popular freedom against Charles I. When hardships are unavoidable they can sustain a man, but once they have passed, after he has had time to understand them with his mind, the pain rises and hurts.

Shakespeare's insight recognized this when he wrote the passage in which Othello, speaking of his first meetings with Desdemona, tells of the desperate strugglings and sufferings of his younger days:

> *'Twas pitiful, 'twas wondrous pitiful:*
> *She wisht she had not heard it: yet she wisht*
> *That heaven had made her such a man: she thanked me;*
> *And bade me, if I had a friend that loved her,*
> *I should but teach him how to tell my story,*
> *And that would woo her. Upon this hint I spake:*
> *She loved me for the dangers I had past,*
> *And I loved her that she did pity them.*

It was so difficult, it was so terribly difficult, to build a community, much less a nation, in Canada's harsh terrain. What wonder when the railroads were built, when the buffalo herds vanished and the Indians were retired to reservations, that a people rapidly becoming middle class should no longer wish to think much about the truth of the early days. Step by step in the nineteenth century, leap by leap in the twentieth, Canadian society has fled from its past.

I think of Sir John Macdonald, still Prime Minister but an old man, sitting on the cow-catcher of one of the first C.P.R. locomotives and travelling in exultation up the Kicking Horse, over the Great Divide into British Columbia. The barrier of those mountains had haunted his entire political life. On the conquest of them had depended his country's survival; Canadians alone had had to build that railway through their own Rockies. On the day when Sir John first rode through, he must have felt like a man who has always been poor, always stretched to the limit, always been required *to prove* that his country had a right to exist, and then suddenly, beyond expectation, knows that at last both he and the country have not quite failed. With the coming of the railways, most of the rivers ceased to be avenues of travel.

Yet even in the present century there have been men who used them as such, just as everyone did in the old days. Charles Camsell was one of these, and he died only in 1958. Born in Fort Liard in the Mackenzie country where his father was a factor in the Hudson's Bay Company, Camsell grew up beside that vast, lonely river of the Northwest Territories nearly two thousand miles away from any organized community. When he went to school he had to go all the way to Winnipeg, a distance of eighteen hundred miles, and he did so by canoe, York boat, Red River cart and his own feet. When his education was over, he spent many years of lonely exploration in the Mackenzie and Yukon regions; he nearly lost his life to a polar bear, to hostile Eskimos and even to hunger. Years later he became Deputy Minister of Mines and Resources, and in this capacity he once flew with Punch Dickins over some of the territory he had covered by canoe and dog team. It was like leaping from the primitive past into the technological future in the span of a few years of life. Camsell remarks, without further comment, that he and Dickins accomplished in two hours a journey which once had taken him half a year.

But the rivers of Canada are still there, and their appearance and character have changed little or not at all in the last century and a half. It is only our use of them that has altered. Now we fly over them, build dams on them, fish in them for sport, and use them for municipal water supplies. We even give them a passing glance when we cross them on government-built bridges or drive beside them at seventy miles an hour.

But the rivers are worth knowing, though none of us will ever know them as the voyageurs did; even though the art of canoe-handling in which Canadians once excelled the world has so vanished in Canada that at the last Olympic Games our few competitors were overwhelmed by Russians from the Dnieper and by Germans and Austrians from the Rhine and Danube. But the memory of the canoes is there, however buried. A great river, after all, is more than a personality in its own right. It is a vital link with a people's past, and also it is a mystery. The eternal river is always a new river yet forever the same; just as men are new in each generation but forever the same, and always must re-learn what the others learned before them. As I did myself, at least up to a point, when I found out that a personal discovery of the rivers of Canada was also a discovery of the country which had given me a home.

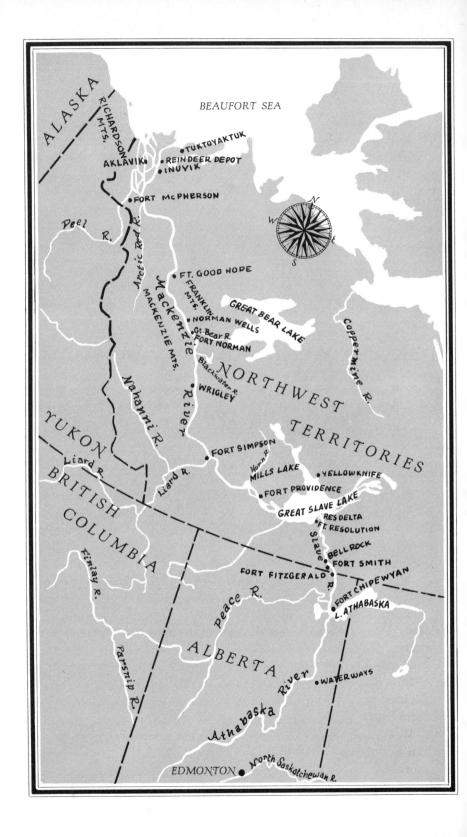

The Mackenzie

The day before I set out for the Mackenzie, I was on the shore of
Nova Scotia facing Sambro Light and watching the Atlantic swing
and ebb in crannies of those granite masses scraped bare by the
glacier and polished by two hundred centuries of wind and water.
In places the eastern coast of Nova Scotia looks as much a product
of the glacier as the habitable parts of Greenland. Where I was
lying was as far east as anyone could go on that parallel of latitude and still be in America. I lay with my back against the continent and watched a white liner that had come up over the horizon
grow large and finally disappear behind the bluff of Chebucto
Head on her way to dock in Halifax. I noticed that she wore the
Greek flag.

Any time now, I thought, I would be leaving for the Mackenzie
River and the idea of doing so still seemed strange to me. It had
always seemed so far away – much, much farther away than any
river in Europe. Only a fortnight ago I had been in England stay-
ing with a friend on the edge of Epping Forest near London, and
we had spread out maps to look at the Mackenzie country. Three
of my friend's children were clustered around in some fascination,
as children usually are in the presence of maps, and one of them
made me promise to send her a picture of Eskimos from the
Mackenzie.

"I'll have to go all the way down to here before I meet any Eskimos," I told her, and my finger came to rest at Aklavik.

The Mackenzie still seemed far away as I drove back to Halifax
late that afternoon drowsy from the sun and the salt air. When I
reached my mother's house, she told me I was wanted long distance by Edmonton and I made a quick calculation. It was six
o'clock in Halifax; in Edmonton it was only two o'clock, so I
decided to wait for half an hour to make sure my caller was back
from lunch.

When the operator put me through, the call was from an official of the Northern Transportation Company which handles the
movement of freight in the Mackenzie region and along the Atha-

baska. He told me a tow of barges would leave the vicinity of Fort Smith inside a week and would proceed down the Slave River, across Great Slave Lake and then go down the lower Mackenzie to Tuktoyaktuk on the Beaufort Sea. There would be accommodation for me on the tugs, I was told, but I was advised to make my own arrangements with Canadian Pacific Airlines for getting out of the country at the end of the run. I was advised to depart for Edmonton immediately.

The next day I drove in my car down Nova Scotia to Digby, where I saw Princess Margaret review a hundred fishermen on the wharf, all of them wearing yellow oilskins and sou'westers although it was a warm day of bright sun. My car was driven aboard the *Princess Helene* and I crossed the Bay of Fundy to Saint John.

The day after this I spent travelling north along the St. John River, crossed the height of land so important to the treaty-makers of 1783, reached the St. Lawrence at Rivière du Loup and had a drink before dinner while looking across the ten-mile width of the St. Lawrence at a majestic sunset over the mountains behind Murray Bay. The next day I drove up the St. Lawrence to Montreal, finishing a journey of about eight hundred miles from Halifax.

Early the next morning I was in a TCA aircraft flying across the country to Edmonton, and at that stage in my discovery of rivers, I knew so little about them that I was unaware that the plane was practically following the course of the voyageurs all the way west from Montreal.

In Edmonton I soon made the discovery everyone makes the moment he has anything to do with the Canadian north. The time-sense I had grown up with ceased to mean anything in a country which, by southern standards, is essentially timeless. I was told the tow down river had been delayed. When would it start? Well, it should start about any time now. I wanted to know precisely when in order to arrange for air transport south from Aklavik, and at that time of the year air transport south did not seem too easy to get, since I would be coming out at the end of the season when the summer workmen would be going home. Well, I was told, it should be starting pretty soon, maybe in three days. How long would it take going down to Aklavik? It shouldn't take too long. It was hard to say, but maybe ten days.

I walked around Edmonton for more than a week, observed the North Saskatchewan in that section of its course, studied

maps and figures about the Mackenzie and called the transportation company every day. One day I went to the races and lost ten
dollars, and when I came back to the hotel that afternoon the
phone rang and I was told to report at Fort Smith the next day.

Edmonton is the most northerly city of any size in Canada,
which means it is the most northerly of any size in North America.
Yet it took the aircraft two hours and forty minutes non-stop to
reach Fort Smith, the administrative centre of the Northwest Territories lying just over the line of demarcation between the Territories and the Province of Alberta. For a little of that journey we
flew over prairie farms, but by far the most of it was over the rough
mat of the northern Canadian bush, with little streams and
myriads of lakes dotting the blackish-green of a forest seen from
the air. It was a wonderful preparation for the Mackenzie none the
less, for we were flying then over the upper basin of the entire
system. So perhaps this is as good a place as any to outline what
the Mackenzie system is, and to show it in relation to other great
river systems of the world.

Most encyclopedias give the total area of the Mackenzie basin
as 682,000 square miles, a region two and a half times the size
of Texas and more than thirteen times larger than England. Later
and more accurate surveys place the figure at about 700,000
square miles, which is really an immense amount of real estate.
In terms of its drainage area, the Mackenzie stands about level
with the Yangtse and quite a bit ahead of the St. Lawrence, Volga
and Zambesi. However, it stands well below the Rio de la Plata,
the Congo, the Mississippi, the Nile and the Lena, and far below
the colossal Amazon with its basin more than two-thirds as big
as the area of the entire continental United States before Alaska
joined the Union.

The Mackenzie marked on the maps is the great river which
issues from a north-westerly bay in Great Slave Lake and flows
down to the north until it reaches the arctic sea 1,200 miles away.
But this final stretch is merely the last outpouring of a system
which begins more than fifteen hundred miles farther south and
from a variety of sources.

The two great tails of the Mackenzie system are the Peace and
the Athabaska, and both flow out of the Canadian Rockies just
east of the Great Divide. In Jasper National Park you can see the
Athabaska purling, bubbling, purple-blue if the sky colour is right,
throbbing down the valley from its source in the Columbia Ice-

field. The young Athabaska is as happy a river as I have ever seen, and even in its stripling reaches it gives you a sense of the power and mastery of the system to which it belongs. It is a strong river as it flows by Jasper determined to have its own way, and a confident river after it has descended from the mountains and begins its long north-easterly course across the Alberta plain. Most of its journey is through wilderness. Though for a time it skirts the northernmost fringe of Alberta settlement, it soon curves on into the vast forest-land of the north. It terminates in Lake Athabaska near Fort Chipewyan, which is surely one of the most historic sites in Canada west of Fort Garry. In his novel of the Mackenzie country, *Where the High Winds Blow*, David Walker has a line expressing what thousands must have felt in the presence of the Athabaska: the whole sense of the North seems to be compressed into its very name. The total length of this tail of the Mackenzie from the Icefield to the lake is seven hundred and sixty-five miles (a distance a little less than the length of the Rhine) and most of these miles are navigable.

But the Mackenzie system has another southern tail even larger, the Peace, which often is listed separately as the fifth longest river in Canada. Its birth is dramatic: it is formed by the head-on collision of the Finlay and Parsnip in one of the wildest and most spectacular regions of the Canadian Rockies. It drives down through rapids and gorges to the plain, and then in calm and majestic solitude it winds northward through the prairie into which the homesteaders moved in the 1920s, and then into the vast northern forest which it shares with the Athabaska. Finally it gives an abrupt turn and completely takes possession of another river — indeed becomes it — and this other river is marked on the maps as the Slave.

The length of the Peace is usually given as 1,054 miles from the forks of the Parsnip and Finlay to its confluence with the Slave. But the Slave, which coils like a smooth, cold, tranquil serpent through a forest wilderness for 310 miles until it empties in Great Slave Lake, is not really a separate river. When Samuel Hearne discovered it in 1771, naming both river and lake after the Slavi Indians of the region, he had come to it from the north-east. He ended his exploration there, and he never knew that what he had called the Slave was simply the final course of a mighty river which had begun more than a thousand miles away in the Rocky Mountains. In freshet, some of the waters brought down by the Peace actually ebb southward up the Slave into Lake Athabaska.

Below Great Slave Lake begins the Mackenzie proper, or the lower Mackenzie, and it is fed steadily all the way down to the sea by a great number of tributaries.

The largest of these is the Liard which rises in Dease Lake in British Columbia near the Pacific and flows for nearly seven hundred miles through wild country until it reaches the Mackenzie at Fort Simpson. Before the entry of the Liard, the Mackenzie water is cleaner even than that of the St. Lawrence just after it leaves Lake Ontario. But the Liard has had a rough journey; it has torn its way through many a mile of sandstone and when it enters the Mackenzie its water, brown with sediment, seems to divide the mainstream into two separate sections. So great is the thrust of the Liard that all the way down to Wrigley the brown Liard water follows the left bank while the clean Mackenzie water is pressed to the right. But the streams meld finally, and thereafter the Mackenzie is stained. The Liard, like the Peace and the Athabaska, is a great stream in its own right, with many tributaries of which the wild Nahanni has tempted more than one adventurer who never returned. It also has a profound effect on the climate of the entire Mackenzie region. Down the valley of the Liard flow warm airs from the Pacific, with the result that Fort Simpson in winter has a climate little colder than that of the Laurentians north of Montreal.

But all the streams entering the Mackenzie from the east are cold, and the coldest of them is the short Great Bear River which drains Great Bear Lake, an inland sea larger than any in the hemisphere except Superior, Huron and Michigan. Great Bear Lake seldom unfreezes before the last week in July and its river is so achingly cold it feels like melting ice. People who have come down the Great Bear River in canoes have told me that when they enter the Mackenzie, the sudden change in air-temperature is equivalent to a journey five hundred miles to the south: the difference, say, between Montreal and Washington on a September day.

The true length of the Mackenzie? Of no other river in Canada does the old question make less sense. The only way to judge the Mackenzie in relation to other rivers is in terms of its drainage basin and its flow; in flow, it ranks seventh in the world, and in the western hemisphere is exceeded only by the Amazon and the Mississippi.

Our aircraft throbbed monotonously northward as I talked with the young man in the next seat. Like nearly everyone else in the plane, he was dressed in work clothes and had a dunnage bag stuffed with metal objects. At first I thought him a prospector, but he told me he was working for the government measuring rivers for velocity. A forgotten memory stirred: in Nova Scotia years before this young man was born, I had spent two weeks doing the same kind of job on a few of the little streams I used to call rivers. The routine, I gathered from the young man, has changed little with the years. You stand in the stream if it is shallow enough, or you cross it by boat or canoe held firmly in a straight line by a cable stretched across the river. You lower into the water a little propeller on the end of a long metal shaft, the current turns the propeller and each turn registers with a click in the earphones attached to the instrument. The propeller must be lowered at a variety of depths. By counting the number of clicks against a stopwatch, and taking a series of readings at different depths all the way across the stream, you can, after averaging out all your readings, estimate the mean flow of a river. The operation must be repeated at a number of stages all the way down the stream and it is less tedious work than it sounds. Most people find it hypnotically restful to stare at moving water.

The young man was talking about the flies: "Last year I never saw anything like them. They lasted all the way through to the fall. One day they got inside my pants and I couldn't get rid of them because I was miles from camp. They bled me so bad my pants stuck to me when I took them off. This year has been a good one for flies. Where you're going, you should find them nearly all gone."

The plane seemed to be beginning a slow descent, but when I looked out I could see no sign of a post or a settlement.

"I tell you, my thighs looked like stewed strawberries. When I'd go out on the job the flies felt like grit in my eyes even when they weren't actually in them. You could hear mosquitoes on tin roofs after dark. It's the mosquitoes in this country — I mind them far worse than the blackflies, though the bulldogs hurt more. Bulldogs can bite clean through a sweater. With ordinary blackflies I've always figured the effect is psychological. If you smear 6-12 on your face they won't bite you, but they'll swarm in a haze right in front of your eyes and follow you around. It generally takes me about two days to get used to them, but there are places I've been up here in the muskeg where the mosquitoes have really scared me."

I asked him if he knew the song written by Wade Hemsworth about blackflies. It had been sung several times over the radio and it seemed to me the most authentic song I had ever heard of the Canadian north:

> *Oh, the blackflies*
> *The little blackflies!*
> *I'll die with the blackflies picking my bones*
> *In north Ontar-eye-o-eye-o*
> *In north Ontar-eye-o!*

"I've been on the job in North Ontario and they're bad, but this country is worse. Maybe it's the permafrost that makes the muskeg so wet when it oozes through in the summer. I don't know what it is exactly, but down river where the Peel comes in, the mosquitoes are supposed to be the worst in the world."

We flew on level over the empty land, and the man leaned across me and pointed: "There's the delta of the Athabaska."

I had seen the young and happy river rise; now I was looking down at the old and experienced river going to its temporary rest in the lake. The delta of the Athabaska looks like the delta of most northern rivers, and is not an excessively large one: a maze of swamps and small channels with some principal threads of broad water which are the main courses of the stream finding their way through the obstacles the river itself has deposited. Out of the flat, brownish-black mat of the delta occasional glitters struck sharply upward as the sun was reflected from water oozing through acres of scrubby bush and marsh grass. We were too high to see the birds, but the whole region seemed mysteriously alive with the energy in it. Even with a single bucket of water, I thought, a child can make a delta. If he pours out his bucket on the sand a few yards from the water's edge, the water he pours will make its own channel just as a river does, and will form a tiny delta an inch or two wide on the verge of the sea.

A new river loomed up and it was the Slave, and after a short while I saw men on the other side staring out, crossed the plane and had a quick glimpse of the Peace coming in from the west. The two great tails of the Mackenzie system were now united, with the so-called Slave taking Athabaska water as well as Peace water. The plane began to descend rapidly and inside a few minutes we were on the air strip at Fort Smith.

Besides the air strip, Fort Smith contains about a thousand inhabitants in summer and a neat little hotel where I was told you can buy your last drink in the northland: below Fort Smith, no liquor unless you bring it in with you. While I was finishing my lunch a man entered, asked for me and told me he would drive me to the Company's work camp at Bell Rock. He was the manager, Joe Burkhart.

We set out in a truck for the camp along the widest dirt road I ever drove on. It went almost dead straight through virgin bush and circumvented the famous rapids of the Slave which begin at Fort Smith and last for about sixteen miles. Now this road extended all the way from Fort Fitzgerald, a total of twenty-six miles. Below Bell Rock, the main Mackenzie system is navigable all the way to the sea.

I asked Joe Burkhart why the road was so wide and was astonished by his answer.

"We have to portage tugboats and barges through here," he said, "broadside on."

The head of steel, I knew, was far south at Waterways on the Athabaska. There the freight, and even the barges and tugs in sections, were conveyed by rail, reassembled and put into the river. They went down the Athabaska to Chipewyan in the lake, then entered the Slave, but the rapids at Smith stopped them. Hence this broad highway in a country which has no other roads of any sort.

"You'll see a boat come over this week," Joe said. "She's in the Athabaska now."

"But they told me I'd be on the river tomorrow."

"Well, I guess it will be a little while yet."

So I waited at Bell Rock for nine days which were a strange mixture of frustration and interest. Here, at least, one could see the modern Canadian North in action, and the whole development depends on the diesel engine. Bell Rock camp, bulldozed out of the bush, contains quarters for the men, a large machine shop, a carpenter's establishment, a radio station, a warehouse the size of what you would expect on the dock of a modest ocean port, and the dock itself in front of which a dredger was moored lifting some of the silt brought down by the river. The Slave at this point looks small because an island faces the camp. North of the camp there is no road at all, nothing but bush for hundreds of miles. There are long, heavy slipways of baulked timber up which the barges and tugs are dragged for the winter, and down which they are pushed into the river in spring. About a hundred men work and eat in the camp all summer long, and in the fall they are flown out.

They eat like kings, but faster. Never have I seen so much food eaten so quickly by so few, and that is the prime difference between the modern Canadian frontier and the old one. Gone are the days of scouse, pork and beans, pemmican, salt codfish and salt pork. The breakfast gong rang at 7:15 every morning, the men rushed into the mess shed and set to, and inside twelve to fifteen minutes the average man managed to work his way through tomato juice, six rashers of bacon, four or five eggs and half a dozen flapjacks soaked with maple syrup, marmalade or jam as the fancy took him. In the middle of the morning there was a coffee break, which meant an extra snack if you wished it. Dinner was just after twelve with hot meats, vegetables and all the pie anyone wanted. Supper was another dinner with hot meats, vegetables and all the pie anyone wanted – in fact, all the anything anyone wanted. At nine o'clock came coffee, tea and cold cuts, as much as anyone could swallow.

In high summer, especially in June, the sun sets very late in Bell Rock and it never really gets dark until summer's end. There is nothing for the men to do after 5:45 but work overtime and digest their meals. This is not the true North of the true arctic men, but the industrial North. Why do the men overeat? I don't know. But they are amicable, they don't quarrel, and the feeling of the North, the subconscious sense that you are far away from normal living, perhaps sheer boredom, stimulates everyone to overeat, with the result that some men put on fifty extra pounds in a season. I used to take long walks along the portage to rid myself of the heavy feeling of too much food. The moment I crossed the rise of ground leading out of the camp, the moment the noise of the diesels disappeared, the immensity of the northern bush closed around me. Prairie chickens skittered about in flocks of a hundred at a time. Once I saw a black bear as heavy with food as the men in the camp, and once when I followed a jeep trail into some muskeg and bush, suddenly the whole land seemed to rise up ahead of me like a huge glossy black umbrella opening up. It was a flock of northern ravens lifting themselves from the Bell Rock dump. Those carrion ravens of the north are almost as large as capons.

A few days later Morris Zaslow came over the portage from Fort Smith in one of the Company's trucks. He was a professor of history at the University of Toronto and he had with him a three-hundred-thousand-word manuscript on the Mackenzie region. He also was going down on the tow, and for the next three weeks we were constant companions.

Naturally we met many of the men in the camp, and they came from a variety of places in Canada and countries of the world. There was Stoni Thorsteinsen whom everyone along the Mackenzie River knew as a good man; for years he had been a steamboat captain and now was in charge of the general river traffic of the company. It was a very pleasant camp, comfortable, not in the least like the tough lumber camps of the east, and on the whole the men seemed content. One man told me he liked northern work because he always had something to look forward to. While he was here, he looked forward to the winter with his family in Vancouver; while he was in Vancouver, he looked forward to getting away from his family and returning to the north. Some of the men read good books. I met a radio operator reading *The Brothers Karamazov* and a chef with a copy of Spinoza, and I remember a carpenter saying to me the prophetic words: "If you ever drink Mackenzie water, you'll always want to come back."

The odd phrase moved me somewhat, for it had an origin in time which the carpenter did not know. Originally the phrase was, "If you ever drink Nile water, you'll always come back." I asked the carpenter if the words were his own or if he had heard them somewhere, and he told me that his first year in the north he had heard them from a Sister of Charity at Fort Norman.

"If you ever drink Mackenzie water," he repeated, "you'll always want to come back."

He loved the lower river, he said, because it made him feel good, and by this he did not mean "feel good" in the sense that Hemingway uses it after a drink, but that it made him feel a good man.

Waiting has always irked me, and nothing makes me feel so tired as idleness, but there was not a thing that Morris and I could do until that tow got under way. It was now well past the middle of August and I had urgent need to be back in Montreal by the end of the first week in September. I fretted. But it is useless to fret against the spirit of a timeless land. Somehow the far Northwest seems to have tamed even the meticulous time-demands of the machines it uses. Also the weather was warm and humid. Though this country can get murderously cold in January – the Slave stays frozen many days after the Liard has unlocked the middle river lower down in the north – in July and August the Fort Smith region is no cooler than Ontario. All of us were issued bed rolls, and I found mine so warm I had to sleep on top of it. Then it rained, and the next day the river silt on which the camp is built turned into a thick rich slime with a fetid odour coming from the acid in it. Wearing rubber boots, Morris and I moved outside with a sliding motion as though we were on skis, and I wondered what the river men had done in this kind of silt when they tracked. The skies were livid and somebody blamed the El Greco tints on atomic explosions in Siberia. They were beautiful, but at times heavy and ominous, and the sense of the vastness of the North, of the viridian of endless forest dense on either side of that slow river, made me feel like a prisoner.

Then came an evening when Morris and I were walking in the clearing and he turned with a cry and pointed. The sun had just broken through clouds over the forest and was streaming horizontally in shafts like searchlights across the camp. At the very end of the portage, on the final rise of ground, we saw emerging out of the forest a white ship, broadside on. It looked huge with the sun smashing against it. I remembered the manager telling me about a ship which was coming down the Athabaska and was going to be portaged. This was it.

"Well," either Morris or I said, "I suppose that's as good an image of the modern North as either of us will ever see."

The ship's presence there was certainly evidence of what the diesel engine has done in these parts. For years this portage by the Fort Smith rapids had been one of the toughest in the whole Canadian river network. It exhausted Mackenzie's party when they made it long ago. In the York boat era they used wooden cradles with wheels under them to carry the boats, and oxen hauled them, though the wretched animals must have been driven mad by the flies, especially by the bulldogs which are notorious here. But now, over the wide road bulldozed out of the bush, even the three-hundred-ton *Radium Dew*, equipped with a radar and echo-sounder, was portaged on trailers hauled by diesel-driven cat tracks. The vessel now emerging was the seventy-five-ton *Dumit*, her job being to check and later to pick up the buoys marking the channels. The next day she was pushed down the slipways and sailed off. Two cat tracks, one in front to haul and the other behind to serve as a brake, and two trailers supported by forty-eight heavy wheels, had portaged the *Dumit* all the twenty-six miles from Fort Fitzgerald in eight hours!

During our time of waiting, eight barges were loaded. The barges were of steel, the smaller ones a hundred and twenty feet long and the larger ones a hundred and fifty, each of them weighing several hundred tons. Two of them were house-barges, but the rest were open, and the cargo was taken aboard by fork-lifts and stacked in sections of the barges according to the destinations for which they were bound. Everything necessary for maintaining life and work in the modern north was included in the cargo: all kinds of canned goods, flour, machine parts, boxes of dynamite, a few bulldozers and jeeps and a number of dog toboggans. There was even a heavy store of fresh oranges in crates bound for Aklavik. The total weight of our eight-barge tow came to 2,600 tons. This single tow of ours moved as much cargo, at least in terms of weight, as could have been carried in the old days by nine hundred *canots du nord*.

Behind this complex operation on the Mackenzie system lies a series of interlocking stories.

For more than a century the Hudson's Bay Company had maintained its lonely little posts up here to take care of the diminishing fur trade. Though it was known that the region abounded in metals, the economic hazard of moving them more than a thousand miles south in a roadless land made most prospectors leave the territory alone. When Gilbert Labine discovered a huge silver deposit on Great Bear in the 1930s he knew it would be economically useless to him; transportation costs of such a heavy metal, which did not bring much price in the market, would far outrun his profits. But on that same expedition Labine discovered pitchblende, and this discovery played its part in changing the history of the world.

At first Labine used his pitchblende solely for the refining of radium, and he hired the barges and stern-wheelers of the Hudson's Bay Company, together with aircraft, to get the raw material out. Then he decided to form his own transportation company, which was the father of the present Crown Company whose guest I was while in the Mackenzie region. Labine had diesel-driven tugs built as far away as Sorel on the St. Lawrence, conveyed them in sections by rail to Waterways on the Athabaska, reassembled them there, and sent them down the Athabaska, through the lake and over the widened portage to Bell Rock. With the outbreak of war the mine on Great Bear became — though it was a top secret at the time — the most important mine in the world. Out of it was taken the uranium which was fissioned over Hiroshima and Nagasaki.

Also with the war came the Japanese attack on the Aleutians followed by the American riposte. The American Army, in co-operation with Canada, built the Alaska Highway and also the pipeline called the Canol Project, the latter intended to convey oil from Norman Wells across hundreds of miles of northern wilderness to a final destination at the Alaskan naval bases. For a few years the empty land roared with activity, and the American Army for a time had as many as 18,000 troops working there. Hundreds of millions of dollars were spent inside a few years. Bulldozers, power shovels, jeeps by the hundreds, refinery equipment, explosives, chemicals and thousands of tons of stores were moved down from the south. Nearly all of it was wasted. Though the Alaska Highway remains and will always be valuable, the pipeline was completed just at the moment when the Japanese threat to the Aleutians disappeared. As the troops went home, bonfires were made of unwanted stores. To this day, the swamps and muskegs are supposed to contain hundreds of bulldozers, power shovels and jeeps driven into them and abandoned. One man at Bell Rock told me there are even some bulldozers on the bottom of Great Slave Lake. They rolled off the barges when a tow was caught in a storm.

Now all this activity has vanished and the land is mostly empty again, and perhaps legends are told of the war days in the teepees at Fort Norman where Indians sit in the summer playing cards while their huskies lie chained and half-starving on the shore. No uranium comes out of Great Bear now that the market is glutted and the mine has been closed. The eternal silence has returned to nearly all the Mackenzie, though the people seldom hear the silence unless they are lost and in trouble, for wherever people are, the sound of the diesel is in their ears. Practically all the cargo goes down the river now and is consumed in the little posts and the D.E.W. Line stations on the shore of the Arctic Ocean. The only thriving town in the region is Yellowknife on the north shore of Great Slave Lake.

At last *Radium King* came up the Slave, and she was beached for a day while men worked on a rudder post damaged by a shoal. Then she was hammered down the slipways by a pair of cats buffeting against the thick hempen mat hung over her side, and Morris and I were told the tow was ready to start.

As this tow was to be our home for many days I should describe how all the Mackenzie River tows are assembled. The barges are yarded together two or three abreast and lashed tightly like bundles of cordwood by heavy hawsers made fast about their bollards. Behind them, hidden (except for its wheelhouse and radar fan) by the piled-up mass of goods, wedged against the pushing posts of the last barge, is the little tugboat thrusting forward like a goat and made especially manoeuvrable by four rudders. From the taffrail of the tug to the front apron of the leading barge of the centre column the distance is about five hundred feet, so that a tow – or rather, a push – of this sort has the length of a sizable ocean-going merchant ship. Astern, the diesel thunders in your ears and the steel decks of the tug throb from the engine and propellers. But up front on a windless day there is no sound but the faint siffle made by flat-bottomed barges coasting along the surface of a river.

There was a pile of dog-toboggans on the apron of the front barge and how many hours I spent sitting on them I have long forgotten. There was nothing to do but sit or scramble about the stacks of goods on the barge, nor anything else I much wanted to do. Hour after hour we went down the vast river system through that savage and colossal terrain. We seemed to be gliding out and on into the pastel colours of sky and water while first the Slave, and later the Mackenzie, overwhelmed us with the grandeur of its monotony, with the utter immensity of its Siberian silence. All the way from Bell Rock to Great Slave Lake – half a day, a night, and then a whole day until sunset – we went down the curving Slave past island after island with the forests on either side, and in all that time we saw not a sign of human habitation. Occasionally we saw a white pelican larger than any swan basking on the river. Sometimes an eagle soared overhead and there were gulls and those ever-present glossy black ravens of the North. Otherwise nothing but the immense low forest of spruce with the occasional splash of white birch, and the immense arching sky with shifting clouds, and the immense, lake-like curves of the lonely river. On and on we went around the curves. Then in the early evening – it was turning to twilight at about 7:45 because we were less than a month from the equinox — we came out of the forest into the delta.

Of all the places I have ever been in my life, I still remember the delta of the Slave — or rather, of the Peace — as the loneliest. Here is loneliness on a scale awe-inspiring, and increased by your knowledge of having seen no habitation for so long. Broad and flat, the marsh grass extends for miles, and there were more wild geese and duck than I had ever believed possible in a single place. We came out of the channel to the edge of the lake which stretched far away into the twilight looking cold and hostile, and in a strong wind it was kicking up a fast, ugly chop. The name they give to this place is Res Delta after Fort Resolution just around the bend of the lake from the river's mouth. (How tell-tale are the names of these Hudson's Bay Company posts in the Canadian North!) There were no ships on the lake, nothing here at all, apparently, but the geese, ducks, pelicans and the muskrats printing V-trails in the water as they swam away from the barges. I had the feeling that I was approaching nothing at all.

I was wrong: we were just about to meet the only known and identifiable human being between Bell Rock and Fort Providence.

He came sculling out to us in a rowboat and he looked like the French philosopher Jacques Maritain with a great shock of white hair, a strangely learned face and a still stranger expression in his eyes. He said only a few words and he did not come aboard. Provisions were handed down to him and he stowed them in his boat, then turned and sculled slowly back to the shore where I saw a pair of husky dogs sitting in front of a tiny shack, their mouths open and their tails bushed around their haunches. Somebody told me the man was employed here as watchman over the barges which often were moored nearby awaiting a change of tugs. I remember thinking he was no watchman of barges, but a watchman over eternity itself.

"You know," a deckhand told me, "that man's lived in Paris and Rome and all over the world. He knows about paintings and books. He told a friend of mine he knows about foreign women."

"What is he doing here?"

"I don't know, but it could be quite a story if anyone did know. He don't like talking. He never goes out. (By 'out' in these parts they mean 'out of the north'.) In the winter he has a job just as lonely as this somewhere else."

"Is he bushed?"

"No, I don't think he's bushed. Not by the bush, anyhow. A man can want to live alone, can't he?"

The remark may have been casual, or it may have been intended as a warning not to ask too many personal questions about people met in the North. I still don't know how it was intended.

Meanwhile there was a small conference in the wheelhouse because the captain had discovered we were entirely cut off from communication with anyone he wanted to talk to. In this country there are no phones except within the camps, no roads, no telegraphs. Radio is used for all messages and they are all sent in clear, with the Bell Rock sender servicing a district several times larger than Germany. The captain, a Japanese-Canadian called Albert Irey, was trying to reach Captain Brinki Sveinson of *Radium Yellowknife* whose ship he had expected to meet here at Res Delta. On Great Slave Lake it is impossible for any tug to push the barges: the heave of the deep water would break their hawsers. On the lake the barges have to be towed in line ahead secured by a heavy steel cable to the power winch at the tug's stern, and the maximum number of barges any tug can handle is four. *Radium King* would take the four smaller barges across; *Radium Yellowknife*, a more powerful ship, would take the four larger ones.

In the wheelhouse Albert was trying to raise the captain of *Radium Yellowknife*, but all he could hear out of the ship's radio was static and gibberish.

"It might be Russia, for all I know," he said and shrugged.

"Russia?"

"We often get Russia here when we can't get our own friends around a few bends of the river. Radio is a funny thing in these parts. There's been a local black-out for several days. Brinki could be within ten miles of us and I couldn't raise him. Anyhow, let's go."

Albert yanked the signal to the engine room, and for the next half hour he unscrambled the barges. Four were moored to the trunks of heavy trees, the other four were secured to the wire cable payed off astern, and in gathering dusk *Radium King* towed her barges out into the lake. Each barge was five hundred feet behind its leader, and the whole length of the tow was now longer than the *Queen Elizabeth*.

I didn't like the look of the lake at all. Those steep, rapid waves of inland seas have always seemed much nastier to me than the long roll of the Atlantic. The *King* was bucking in the head-sea throwing water and the water was very cold. Above the wheelhouse the radar fan revolved, but the screen was blank except for four dots astern, which were our barges, and the line of the lakeshore we were leaving. The wind drummed hard.

"How much water does she draw?" I asked Albert.

He flashed me a quick smile caught in the light of the binnacle: "About three and a half feet."

"She'll roll," I muttered, knowing how easily I get seasick.

"By the time the night's out maybe you'll think up another word for what she does."

The helm was put over, the *King* began a long, slow turn into the cross sea and the movement began.

"I think I'd better say good-night."

Clutching the guard rail I went down the ladder to the main deck, then I was nearly thrown down the next ladder into the cuddy where we slept. I swallowed a gravol, felt my head spinning and lay down on a cot with my clothes on.

I have been in a north Atlantic gale when the old *Empress of Britain* — the big one bombed to death in the war — shipped it green and solid over her sixty-foot-high fo'c'sle head. Once I spent five and a half hours on a ferry between Dover and Boulogne on a day when the weather was so bad that an English paper described it in a headline which later became famous: STORM OVER CHANNEL CONTINENT ISOLATED. On both those occasions I was deathly sick, but this night on Great Slave was worse. The *King* did not roll: balanced on the weight of her diesels, she flicked back and forth like a metronome trying to keep time to a czardas.

With eyes closed I reflected that Great Slave Lake, after all, is not a sea but a part of a river system. A little later with eyes open I remembered what had happened to the tug *Clearwater* the previous year on Lake Athabaska. Caught in a sudden storm, her captain had tried to shelter behind an island, but when he turned, the towing cable destroyed all his mechanical advantage in the water and the hammering waves capsized his ship. An air search found her the next day serving as anchor to her four barges, but all hands were lost. Then I remembered a story I had heard at Bell Rock about a war-time tow on Great Slave when the barges were carrying carbide and dynamite. The storm struck suddenly as storms do there, and as the water washed over the barges it ignited the carbide. The tugboat captain saw the flames in the night, cut his tow and ran for it. He was three miles away when the dynamite went up, but even at that distance the shock wave was strong enough to knock him off his feet.

Then I became so dizzy I didn't care what happened and somehow I dozed off. I woke with a crash, found myself on the deck half-standing against the side of the ship, thought she was going over and plunged for the ladder. I got on deck, seasickness forgotten, with a life-jacket in my hand, but there was no cause for alarm. The little *King* was flicking back and forth, the water was going over her scuppers, but I realized this was no storm. It was merely a dirty cross-sea working against a ship with only three and a half feet of draught. I went up to the wheelhouse and Albert was still there.

"We're getting along all right, but the wind's freshening. Still no sign of Brinki. It looks as if he's stayed on the other side. The wind may have been heavier over there. If he was out, we should have picked him up on the radar."

When I got back to the bunkhouse I found out what had thrown me out of my bed. The rolling had smashed one leg of my cot. It was impossible to repair it in this weather, so I lay down aslant and tried to get some sleep. It was a bad night and my back was in a partial spasm as a result of being thrown.

The next day the weather was easier, the dizziness wore off and we might just as well have been at sea, for no land was in sight. We moved steadily on at a speed of about four knots towing the barges, and then in a dead calm we approached land where, in a maze of islands, the lower Mackenzie issues from the Lake. The place is called Wrigley Harbour, but there is no habitation there, not even a shack so far as I can remember.

There was also no sign of *Radium Yellowknife* and our radio was still blacked out. Morris and I both knew the *King* was overdue at Yellowknife across the lake, and we took it for granted we would have to sleep in the open on the barges while we waited for our next tugboat.

"I guess Brinki must have gone over on a wider course," Albert said. "Otherwise we'd have caught him on our radar. He's probably coming back from Res Delta now. He should be here by 9:00 tomorrow morning."

I wondered if he would be, for in the North nothing ever seems to happen on schedule. Nor can anyone afford to mind. Storms on the lake are sudden, and so are frosts in the spring and fall. Last June *Radium King* had been frozen into the middle of the lake for ten days. Albert had the patience of the North which I lacked, as well as its valid optimism.

But we did not have to sleep in the open after all, for there was a dredger working in a swamp on the far side with a houseboat where the men slept. After securing his barges to trees, Albert sailed across and we glided up to a cluster of men waiting to welcome us in a haze of blackflies. Four of the men were big-muscled Indians and two of the white men had not shaved for days. The eyelids of one of them were red and swollen from fly bites and he did not even bother brushing the flies off his face when they settled. They took us aboard without question as people always take in strangers in the North. The captain said there were two empty cots, one in the houseboat and the other in the wheel-house of the dredger. Morris and I tossed; he won the houseboat and I the wheelhouse, and as both of us were tired we turned in. The last thing I saw that night was the riding light of *Radium King* fading out as she sailed over the horizon of the Lake.

I woke at dawn wondering where I was, for a bright light was in my eyes. Never before or since have I seen such a sunrise. The sky over the river and land was a flat roof, livid and sinister, and it lay oppressively. In the east a blaze of orange had torn a jagged rent in the sky and the sunrise poured through between sky and water like a searchlight gone mad. It tore another rent in the west and travelled on into a sea of golden glory and the whole sky took fire all at once. A minute before it had been like the sky painted by El Greco over Toledo; now it was Turner's sky over the Thames estuary – but bigger, lonelier, more awe-inspiring. Then with sav-age and unnatural abruptness both holes in the sky closed, the fire died out and it was almost dark, and I saw the shadow – not the reality but the shadow – of an arrowhead of geese flash along the dim surface of the water.

For millions of years spectacles like these have occurred at this section of the river, watched by creatures no more sentient than mosquitoes, blackflies, bulldog flies, gulls, geese, ducks, ravens, pelicans, eagles, moose and bear. What lay to the north-west I did not yet know, but I knew already that the nearest man behind me to the south was that white-haired hermit at Res Delta. In a mo-ment of panic – the noun is accurately chosen – I wondered if human beings are necessary on this earth. Here was this colossal land, here this wild beauty, here this huge inland sea to the south feeding the great river that poured for twelve hundred miles through the wilderness to the world's most useless ocean above the Antarctic. What did the Creator want it all for?

I went back to my cot, shivered a little in my bed roll and woke half an hour later with the breakfast gong ringing.

After breakfast I smoked a cigarette with the machinist, an elderly man with a lined face, and asked him if he liked it here.

"You don't *like* it," he said. "The boat drops you and goes away, and the door is closed on you. We haven't been off this dredge for months. There's no place to go. But I keep coming back. For me it's a good life. For the fellows who've had trouble outside – I wouldn't say I was one of them – the north is a good place."

I asked him how many people lived along the river between Fort Smith and Aklavik in the Mackenzie delta.

"Maybe about five thousand Indians spread around. A few white men in Norman Wells stay the winters to keep the refinery up. A few more here and there at the posts."

The decks of the houseboat swarmed with flies. The dredger cut loose and went to work in the river and Morris and I sat in the bunkhouse and read. There was no sign of *Radium Yellowknife* and the chef told us the radio was still blacked out. It was the only thing he said all day. After the midday meal a breeze rose and took off the flies, so Morris and I borrowed fishing rods and walked a little distance along the shore and began casting. We saw many fish rising, but none rose to our spoons.

This is one of the most stirring sections along the whole system. Here, where the Mackenzie proper begins, the river slides cold and clean off the top of Great Slave Lake at a velocity of five knots with whorl-like eddies and rising fish, and at once it becomes absolutely fierce and masterful. All the sediment brought down by the Athabaska has been scattered to the bottom of Lake Athabaska; all brought down by the Peace to the bottom of Great Slave Lake. Here the system renews itself in a smooth, fast volume of water which aeons ago carved a great twisting trench down to the north. Here was the place, if any, to remember the first of Alexander Mackenzie's great voyages of exploration.

All through the winter of 1789, Mackenzie had stayed at Fort Chipewyan studying the maps of Peter Pond, who was sure a great river flowed from the far side of the Lake. Peter Pond was then becoming an old man and he was willing, with an absence of jealousy rare for an explorer, to turn over this final exploration to a younger man. There can be no doubt that he hoped that *la grande rivière en bas* would turn out to be the Northwest Passage. When he returned to Montreal in 1788, Pond told a friend that he had arranged for another man "to go down the river and from thence to Unalaska and so to Kamschatka and thence through Russia to England." The other man was the young Alexander Mackenzie, a native of Stornoway in the Island of Lewis, and at that time a partner in the North West Company. Mackenzie travelled across the continent in the summer of 1788 and reached Chipewyan before the waters froze. He had no illusions that this voyage into the total unknown would be an easy one, and he set out the moment the ice had broken in the river.

On June 3, 1789, he records in his journal, "we embarked at nine o'clock in the morning at Fort Chipewyan . . . in a canoe made of birch bark. The crew consisted of four Canadians, two of whom were attended by their wives, and a German; we were accompanied also by an Indian, who had acquired the title of English Chief, and his two wives in a small canoe, with two young Indians; his followers in a small canoe. These men were employed to serve us in the twofold capacity of interpreters and hunters. This Indian was one of the followers of the chief who conducted Mr. Hearne to the Coppermine River, and has since been a principal leader of his countrymen."

English Chief was to turn out less useful to Mackenzie than was expected, but his voyageurs, whom he drove hard, have surely earned the right to have their names remembered. They were François Barrieu, Charles Ducette, Joseph Landry, Pierre De-Lorme and John Steinbruick.

On the first day Mackenzie made thirty-six miles which brought him to the place where the Peace joins, or rather becomes, the Slave, and there they stopped because they were at the head of the rapids now circumvented by the road from Fort Fitzgerald to Bell Rock. The next day they rose at 3 a.m., portaged six times and camped at 5:30 p.m. in a state of exhaustion. The weather was the unpleasant mixture of snow, sleet and winds — and the winds were against them — which it often is at the beginning of a so-called Canadian spring. But once clear of the rapids, they reached Great Slave Lake in less than four days with the wind against them all the way. In short, Mackenzie's canoes took little more than twice the time to reach Res Delta from Bell Rock in bad weather than *Radium King*, travelling day and night at seven knots steady, had done in the windless weather of late August days.

They found Great Slave Lake still frozen except near the shore, but Mackenzie led his men out into it, and shifted from island to island along the shore, not taking the direct route in deep water as the modern tugs do. The winds were high and sometimes of gale force, and it was not until June 23 that they reached the mainland. It was the harshest possible going. "Though the weather was far from warm," Mackenzie writes, "we were tormented, and our rest interrupted, by the host of mosquitoes that accompanied us." But though they had reached the mainland they had still not found the river, and it was June 29 before they did.

Twenty-six days from Chipewyan to Wrigley Harbour; ahead of them, though they did not know it yet, lay 1,200 miles down to the sea and the long return if they were to get back to Chipewyan before the waters froze. But at first Mackenzie was delighted, for the great river did not run north, but drove westerly for three hundred miles. The Northwest Passage? By July 10 he was almost certain that this river was not the Northwest Passage, but the River of Disappointment, for his latitude (67° 47′) was much too far north for his hopes. "It was evident that these waters emptied themselves into the Hyperborean Sea; and though it is probable . . . that we could not return to Athabaska in the course of the season, I nevertheless determined to penetrate to the discharge of them."

That this young Scot was a rare leader is proved by what he forced his men to accomplish. Though Mackenzie took time to leave the river and climb the mountains which bear his name (his purpose being to inspect the country) he was in the delta by July 12. Two days later, on July 14, 1789, he set up a post on Whale Island in the Arctic and was observing the habits of the coastal Eskimos. It was the very day, though of course he knew nothing about this, that the Paris mob captured the Bastille and started the French Revolution.

Mackenzie's voyage down the great river was not as remarkable a feat as his later journey through the Rockies to the Pacific, but it is certainly one of the great chapters in the long epic of the voyageurs. Were the record not beyond doubt, I would be unable to believe the time made by those canoes. On June 29 Mackenzie left Great Slave Lake at a point very close to the place where Morris and I fished that afternoon beside the houseboat. Yet he was in the vicinity of Aklavik within two weeks and in salt water in sixteen days! The flow of the river is strong, and with favouring winds he sometimes could hoist a sail. But he and his men had to sleep at night and the channels of the river to a man who does not know them can often be confusing. The great river of the North tends to run in a long series of lake-like reaches of about three miles in length with a turn at the end. It could not have been easy always to find the quickest channel to the vital curve, for there are thousands of islands in the stream. Besides, all this journey was made in the face of grim warnings from Indians met on the course that the Eskimos at the river's end would kill them. At Great Bear Lake an Indian told Mackenzie "that it would require several winters to reach the sea, and that old age would come upon us before the period of our return."

But return he did: one hundred and two days after his departure from Chipewyan, he was back at the fort. On the afternoon when I stood beside that cold slide of water dipping off the surface of Great Slave Lake I knew that Mackenzie had accomplished this feat, but I did not yet understand what it had involved.

For I had yet to see the rapids which Mackenzie described with precision as seething with a noise like a kettle. The Providence Rapids, the Green Island Rapids, the Clearwater Rapids do not toss and tumble like those at Lachine or the Long Sault; they swirl at depth and at a speed sometimes as high as twelve knots, and when you look at them the whole surface of the river seems to be quivering. The tugboats cannot control more than four barges at a time in water so swift, so they split their tows and relay them through, mooring four barges at the head of each rapid, taking four down and then returning against the current to recover the remaining four. It took *Radium Yellowknife* barely an hour to take four barges down the Providence Rapids; with her thousand horsepower engine making her plates shudder, it took her more than three hours to hammer her way back running light. Below the entrance of the Blackwater River is a fast stretch sixty miles long, and it took Captain Peterson in *Radium Charles* more than twelve hours to butt back against it. Below Norman Wells is the most spectacular section of the entire stream — the Ramparts, where the river pours satin-smooth and fast at a depth of two hundred feet through high limestone cliffs forming a canyon seven miles long, the sides of the cliffs virtually sheer.

The man who led this famous voyage of discovery has always

seemed to me one of the most interesting and attractive person-
alities in Canadian history; in my opinion, this man is a giant
among our people. His discoveries brought him no credit from his
partners in the Company; jealousy, which the Swedes call the
royal vice, has always been the explorer's sin. But when Mackenzie's voyages were done he crossed the sea and visited London.
There, with the help of a ghost writer whose formal style is mar-
vellously unsuited to the material, he published a book with one
of the longest titles in English letters: *Voyages from Montreal, on
the River St. Lawrence, through the continent of North America,
to the Frozen and Pacific Oceans; in the years 1789 and 1793,
with a preliminary account of the rise, progress and present state
of the fur trade in that country.*

In one of the most brilliant periods in English history, this book
made Mackenzie a celebrity in English society. The young fur-
trader, fresh from the canoes and teepees of Indians, moved with
perfect ease in salons filled with men whose names shine in the
history books. This was also a very exciting time, for Mackenzie
was in London in the period between Nelson's victories at the Nile
and at Trafalgar. Yet the hitherto unknown voyageur made his
place there. The leaders of the land read his book; he was given
a title by the Crown; he was patronized by a Royal duke; he was
painted by the King's Painter-in-Ordinary.

In the context of his life on the Canadian rivers, the personality
revealed by the brush of Sir Thomas Lawrence is almost startling.
There is nothing rough or rugged in the face of this man who
explored one of the roughest and ruggedest terrains in the world.
In the countenance of Simon Fraser there is a stubborn, animal-
like expression, but not in Mackenzie's. This pork and pemmican
eater, this man who could drink under the table most of his fellow
members of the Beaver Club in Montreal, certainly has an obstin-
ate chin. But his face might be a poet's. His eyes, as Lawrence saw
them, are quite marvellous: longing, headstrong, gentle, defiant,
civilized yet making you think of an eagle. The lines put by Ten-
nyson in the mouth of Ulysses apply well to the personality revealed by Sir Thomas Lawrence:

> *Yet all experience is an arch where through*
> *Gleams that untravelled world, whose margins fade*
> *Forever and forever as I move . . .*

With a drop in the wind the flies swarmed back, and Morris

and I went back inside the houseboat. Monotonously the afternoon wore on and I wondered if we would ever get out of this place. I was becoming wearier and wearier of these endless northern delays which always seemed inevitable. Once a bush plane flew overhead, but every time we scanned the horizon the lake was empty. Then, just after sunset, Morris rose quietly, looked out the porthole and said: "Cheer up! The tow is arriving."

Half an hour later we were aboard *Radium Yellowknife* talking to Captain Brinki Sveinson. While we had been tossing in the lake he had sheltered behind an island, not because he thought the lake dangerous for his ship, but because he had an empty vessel in tow which lacked ballast, and he was afraid she might capsize. He told us he would take us down river for two and a half days to his rendezvous with *Radium Charles*, which would in turn take us down to Norman Wells and another rendezvous with *Pelican Rapids*.

The next day our voyage down the Mackenzie began, and it took us longer to reach the Wells from Wrigley Harbour with our eight barges than it would take a modern liner to reach Southampton from New York. Hour after hour, day after day, night after night we passed down the curves and the islands into an ever-increasing sense of sheer immensity. The little posts lie from a hundred to a hundred and fifty miles apart, and nothing human is between them. The first post was Fort Providence where, in the year of Confederation, the sisters at the Catholic mission nearly starved to death. Then come Fort Simpson, Wrigley, Fort Norman, Norman Wells, Fort Good Hope, Arctic Red River, Fort McPherson, Aklavik, Reindeer Depot and Tuktoyaktuk (known on the river as Tuk or Tuk-Tuk) on the fringe of the Arctic Ocean. Because the river supplies all these posts with heavy freight, because there are no roads to supplement it, the Mackenzie system is the only one left on the continent which fulfils the old role all the great rivers once played. In one sense a Mackenzie voyage is like a journey into the past. This is the sole avenue of heavy traffic in a length of more than fifteen hundred miles, nor has the river changed in any important respect since the year when Alexander Mackenzie discovered it. Even the lignite beds he saw burning at Fort Norman burn there still.

Monotony, endless monotony and vast skies, but not a monotony which is depressing. Now the river thrusts fiercely along its trench and scoops great gouges out of the escarpments along the curves; now it flows silent and wide past swamps lined with willow trees; always it embraces islands. We sailed through the wide mirror of Mills Lake and the 3,000-foot-high whale-back of the Mackenzie Mountains emerged on the left, then the Franklin Mountains on the east. The mountains abruptly marshal the stream northward in the great curve now known as the Camsell Bend. I noticed the nights getting longer and cooler. On the first of September there was a frost in the night, fog in the morning and a great movement of wild geese flying south.

I cannot remember one day from the other, but I do remember that the radio was still blacked out when *Radium Yellowknife* was approaching its rendezvous with *Radium Charles*. A deckhand told me he could fetch Australia, but could not hear a thing from the *Charles*; he may have been kidding me about Australia, but I certainly know we picked up Russia one afternoon. Finally Captain Sveinson moored his barges and told Morris and me that he must return up river. The season was late and he could afford to waste no more time. He said he would be willing to keep us on board if we wished, but if he did so he would be unable to transfer us to a northbound vessel. However, he was sure *Radium Charles* would appear some time that day, and that it would be safe for us to wait for it on the barges.

So Morris and I stayed with the barges, *Radium Yellowknife* disappeared around the bend and we were alone on the river in total silence. I thought I saw a bear peering down at us from the top of the escarpment, but it turned out to be a broken, weather-worn tree stump. Then it began to rain and get cold. Wet, feeling what a psychologist would call a sense of insecurity, I walked about among the bales on the barges getting steadily colder. We pried open the door of one of the covered barges and looked for a place to sit. It was jammed to the walls with crates and boxes, but there were two boxes with barely room for both of us, so we sat down and I lit a cigarette. I was just beginning to enjoy it when Morris let out a chuckle and said: "Have you noticed what we're sitting on?" My box was labelled "Dynamite" and his "Dynamite Caps", so I tossed the cigarette over the edge of the barge and just sat. A little before dusk *Radium Charles* emerged around the bend pushing the remainder of our barges.

And so down the river to Norman Wells, the most substantial community of them all because it is not a Hudson's Bay Company trading-post but a little refinery town, the farthest north of any refinery in America. Here the Mackenzie swings out in a magnificent bight, the mountains afford a large plain on either side of the stream and the prospect is one of the finest on the continent. There are homes with gardens growing delphinium eight feet high, technicians and chemists and all the men necessary to keep a refinery in operation. The Wells lie just south of the Arctic Circle and have the last air strip in this part of the North. Below them down to Tuk all the planes are equipped with pontoons and land on the water.

Below the Wells the Mackenzie, having taken in many tributaries with a few more to come, carves almost directly down to the North. In summer the melting of the top layer of the permafrost turns the banks into a kind of slime and in winter the whole region would be locked in total darkness for a month were it not for the gleam of the stars on the snow and the light of the aurora. One old northern hand told me that he once was under a winter aurora so intense his dogs refused to work. The lights kept shifting first to one side then to the other, throwing the dogs' shadows as rapidly back and forth as the *Radium King* in a cross sea, so that the dogs whimpered, lay down and buried their heads in the snow. Below the Wells the contrasts along the Mackenzie are so extreme they can best be described in this sentence: the river enters a land of midnight sun in June and of midday night in December.

Finally this river enters one of the most enormous deltas in the western hemisphere, a fantastic region of submerged and emergent islands, of confused channels, of low banks slimy in summer from a permafrost several hundred feet deep out of which the occasional pingoe pops up, a wonderful country for muskrats and mosquitoes, and at the end of it the true arctic tundra at last. The delta extends north and south a distance of a hundred miles and its seaward spread is seventy miles, with the steep scarp of the Richardson Mountains rising abruptly out of the delta plain, while the easterly section is bounded by the low humped range of the Caribou Hills. Streams ramify here, and only from the air is it possible to visualize the complexity of the channels. The Peel, a sizable and partially navigable river, enters the delta in such a way that some of its lower stretches are easily confused with the master stream. Fort McPherson is located on the Peel, and on one of its channels stands Aklavik, or what remains of it after the community was shifted to Inuvik a few years ago. Here live

Eskimos and a few white men. The permafrost is so near to the surface that when houses are built they use steam hoses in place of drills, and find glare ice at a depth of a few feet. Yet in prepared soil on top of the permafrost, cabbages the size of basket-balls have been grown under the perpetual sun of summer. Inuvik, the most northerly community in the hemisphere, has a latitude about the same as that of Norway's North Cape, but the sea it confronts is colder.

When winter comes to this region it does not come slowly; it strikes with a crack. I met a veteran of many years on the Mackenzie who told me that he once escaped having to spend an entire long winter in Aklavik by a matter of a minute. His was the last plane out, and as he stood on one of its pontoons filling his tank with gas, he suddenly noticed ice forming on the water. He threw the can away, jumped into the pilot's seat without even taking time to screw on the cap of the gas tank, gunned the plane and took off. The thin ice was crackling about the pontoons before he became airborne, and as he made his circle to head south he saw pack ice thrusting in and the lagoon from which he had risen turn opaque as though the frost had cast a wand over it.

Like nearly everyone else who goes down north along the Mackenzie, I flew out, and the usual time of flight from the delta back to Edmonton is roughly eight hours. In my case the flight was much longer because of a variety of delays at some of the posts along the way, and one of these may be worth mentioning because it shows how primitive much of the region still is.

At Norman Wells, where the air strip has been bulldozed out of the bush and has no tarmac, where the planes take off in a cloud of dust, dip below the escarpment and then swoop upward in a wide curve above the river, the airline agent found a man asleep in one of the back seats. He was an Indian who had got on the day before at Fort Smith with a ticket for Hay River on the south shore of Great Slave Lake. Though he had never been in a plane in his life, he immediately fell sound asleep and was still asleep when the plane reached the Wells and the other passengers got out. Nobody noticed him and when he woke in the night the plane doors were locked. Since there was nothing he could do, the man fell asleep again and was still asleep when the rest of us got aboard to fly back south. That Indian, at least, understood that the true North is timeless.

People often ask what future the Mackenzie region has, and I do not think it requires much sense of prophecy to predict that a century from now this river valley will have a large population. By that time, unless there has been a nuclear war, the number of people in the world will be many times what it is now, and any part of the globe with vacant land will seem very attractive. I have a notion that in the east we think of the Mackenzie much as Londoners thought of the St. Lawrence a century and a half ago, as a place picturesque, cold but virtually useless.

But the valley of the Mackenzie in many sections, unlike the muskeg of the Northwest Territories between Great Bear Lake and Hudson Bay, could easily be developed for settlement. The tributaries alone could furnish power to supply more hydro-electricity than is bred today out of the entire St. Lawrence system. The technological revolution which is transforming the Canadian North could function with greater ease in the Mackenzie Valley than in any other part of the new Canadian frontier. After all, the Mackenzie does not become truly arctic until it has reached the delta. A century hence, and probably sooner, there will be many factories along this river. Small though it is, Norman Wells today is a modern, efficient refinery.

But will people wish to live there? Under certain conditions I think so, for most of the ones I met there like it now. Charles Camsell remarked that people either hate the North excessively or love it excessively, and I suppose the same person can feel within him alternate waves of both these emotions. I know that I did. But the man at Bell Rock who told me that if you ever drink Mackenzie water you will want to return said a simple truth. I was glad to get into the country, glad to get out of it, and want to return. The manager at the Wells told me that some of his employees and their families hate the country in their first year and apply for transfers out. But some of those who do go out, a few years later write the company begging to be sent north again. I have never met a true arctic hand who does not yearn to go back.

Three measures will have to be taken before this region can become habitable for a large number of people. The acids in the earth will have to be neutralized, compost will have to be worked into the soil, and the insects will have to be conquered. At various times I have referred to the insects here, but always I return to them, for they are the curse of the whole north country. Whether they are any worse than in Ungava and Rainy Lake I do not know from personal experience, but everyone I met who has travelled widely in the Canadian bush says that here they are the worst of all.

Insects are a plague even to the tugboat crews, and the chef of *Radium King* described them well:

"Insects love a bright surface, and when these tugs with their white upperworks put into the posts in June and early July, I've seen them covered with a quivering, browny-black fur of mosquitoes and blackflies. Hellish is the only word for them in swarms like that. If you breathe without your face being covered by netting, they'll choke you. I've spent hours washing them off the ship with hoses. The drowned ones have blocked my scuppers and I've had to dig them out to let the water go through."

That the insects can be conquered ultimately seems certain, but not by spraying with D.D.T. There are so many thousands of water surfaces in the Canadian north that you could never cover them all, nor could you keep the backflies from breeding in running streams. The only solution seems to be biological, and several scientists have surveyed sections of this country with a view to applying methods of destroying the fertility of flies. But at the moment, with the Mackenzie region costing the country more to keep open than it can return in any form of goods and services, there is not sufficient need to inaugurate a thorough fly-killing programme.

Though I do not expect that anyone a hundred years hence will be reading these words, it amuses me to send them on through time with this prophecy. In the year 2,061 there will be at least three million people living in the Mackenzie Valley. There will be hospitals, schools and at least two universities established on sites overlooking that cold, clean river. After all, it was little more than a century ago that the money of a friend of Alexander Mackenzie himself was used to establish the first university on the banks of the St. Lawrence.

The St. Lawrence

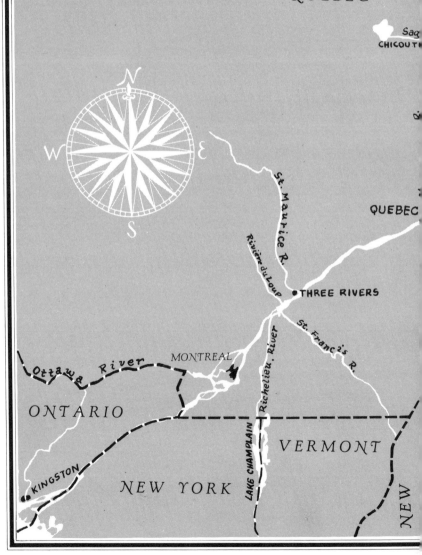

The St. Lawrence

QUEBEC

Sag
CHICOUTI

QUEBEC

St. Maurice R.

Rivière du Loup

●THREE RIVERS

St. Francis R.

Ottawa River

MONTREAL

Richelieu River

ONTARIO

VERMONT

LAKE CHAMPLAIN

KINGSTON

NEW YORK

NEW

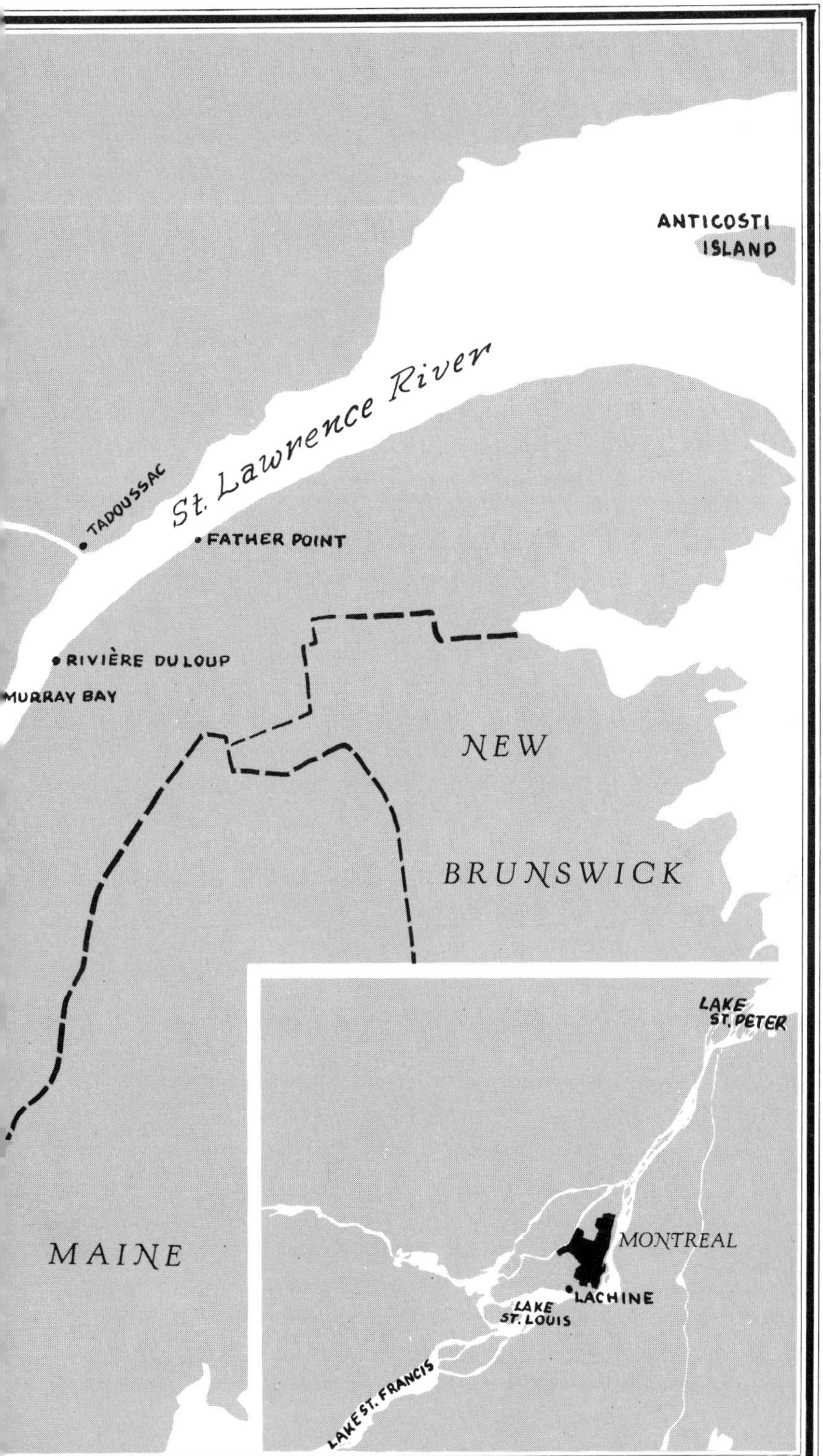

ANTICOSTI
ISLAND

St. Lawrence River

• TADOUSSAC

• FATHER POINT

• RIVIÈRE DU LOUP

MURRAY BAY

NEW

BRUNSWICK

MAINE

LAKE
ST. PETER

MONTREAL

• LACHINE

LAKE
ST. LOUIS

LAKE ST. FRANCIS

To think of the St. Lawrence as a separate entity in a book of this nature is impossible; leaving out the Colorado and the Rio Grande, its story is connected with that of every other river in North America west of the Appalachians. It was the St. Lawrence that led the explorers to all of them. It was to the St. Lawrence that they returned with their furs and the news of their discoveries. It was into the St. Lawrence that the men and the supplies were brought, over it that the armies battled.

So much is known of the St. Lawrence that it is unnecessary to discuss it in the same detail as the Mackenzie. Yet this best-known river, like so many other basic influences in Canada, is remarkably taken for granted. As happens with all great river systems, the experts differ somewhat about its dimensions. But the old question "How long is it?", while unimportant in itself, in the case of this river is well worth asking, because it serves as a pointer to some of the strange and distinctive aspects of the system as a whole.

The St. Lawrence drainage basin is the third largest in North America, its area generally computed at 365,000 square miles. But the St. Lawrence is underestimated by a figure such as this because it contains a feature unique among the rivers of the world: the five Great Lakes which are a part of it.

The total area of the Great Lakes comes to 95,000 square miles. If they were not reservoirs transferring their excess volume into one another and finally into the river — if all that water, navigable from the river, were in motion down a channel — the St. Lawrence would make the Amazon look like a trout stream.

For the Great Lakes contain an immense body of water. The maximum depth of Superior is 1,302 feet; of Huron 750; of Michigan 923; of Erie 210; of Ontario 774. The lakes are set in the land in a series of four tiers. Superior's height above sea level lies between 602 and 623 feet, which means that most of the area of its bottom is well below the level of the surface of the sea. The reason why the surface height varies is pressure of the winds, which on occasion can force the lake's water against one shore while the surface in another section is depressed; it is wind, not the attraction of the moon, which has led many people to believe that Lake Superior has a tide. Huron and Michigan share the second tier at a height of 580 feet. Erie, on the third tier, has a height of 572. The height of Ontario at the point where it overflows into the channel of the St. Lawrence proper is 245 feet.

These drops from tier to tier are extremely gentle except in the region between Erie and Ontario; there the Niagara which links them rushes east in a furious rapid to plunge over its falls. But along the forty-mile-long St. Mary between Superior and Huron the total drop is only thirty feet at the most, while Lake St. Clair and the St. Clair River drop only eight feet between Huron and Erie. As for the river proper, the drop from its egress at the eastern end of Lake Ontario until it merges with the sea is only 246 feet.

These figures explain why the St. Lawrence system has become the greatest inland traffic avenue the world has ever known. Were it not for the rapids it would have been too good to be true, for nowhere else has nature made travel and transport easier for restless man. The lower St. Lawrence flows with just enough velocity not to be sluggish, and only in its rapids with too much velocity to be navigable. So wide is its channel, so even its flow, that in spring freshet it never floods higher than ten feet unless piles of ice act as dams to its current. For these reasons, no less than the fact that it leads directly through the gap between the Appalachian and Laurentian chains, it is no wonder that the St. Lawrence has become the beating heart which sustains so much of North American industry and commerce, with cities like Chicago, Cleveland, Detroit, Toronto, Montreal and Quebec supported by it, with grain and ore floating through it in such quantity that even before the International Seaway was built, the traffic on the St. Lawrence system was more than double that of the Rhine and five times that of Suez.

But how much of the St. Lawrence system can truly be called a river?

The geographers, measuring its length, usually start with the little river St. Louis which rises near the headwaters of the Mississippi and drains easterly into Lake Superior. Calculating a line through the heart of the Great Lakes and the central channels of their inter-connecting streams, and then down the main channel to the Gulf in the region of Anticosti, they come to a figure of 1,900 miles. But there are some two hundred other streams beside the little St. Louis which drain into Lake Superior. And the lake, after all, is largely a reservoir.

According to the definition which says that a river is "any natural stream of fresh water which flows in a well-defined channel", I do not see how anyone can deny that the St. Lawrence is the shortest stream of great importance in the whole of Canada. It can easily be proved that it is shorter than the St. John.

For consider its course. It becomes a true river only where the channel leaves Lake Ontario and enters the bay of the Thousand Islands. From this point to Quebec City the distance is slightly under 400 miles. Though the "river" certainly continues for many miles below Quebec, the moment the stream has embraced the Ile d'Orléans its waters cease to be entirely fresh. The pulse of the distant Atlantic thrusting into the Gulf through Cabot Strait is felt even at Trois Rivières. At Ile d'Orléans, a full 650 miles away from Cabot Strait, tides have often been recorded as high as nineteen feet. Ocean fish abound in the river between Murray Bay and Rivière du Loup, and though the water here is fresh to some extent, there is true seaweed along the shores. Therefore I would say that this majestic reach of the lower river, steadily widening until at the estuary the width is ninety miles, is not a river at all, but what in Scotland is called a firth.

But no matter what the name we apply to it, how incomparable the St. Lawrence is! Clean, alive, sky-blue it comes out of Lake Ontario into its great, driving curve with the thrust of the Lakes behind it. It comes tumbling through the Galops and the Long Sault into the tranquillity of Lake St. Francis; then, after another smooth passage it reaches the Soulanges; then into the calm bight of Lake St. Louis; then through Lachine past Montreal and soon into the ten-mile-wide swell of Lake St. Peter where hundreds of thousands of wild duck breed, and people live a semi-aquatic life in the little bayous; then deep and strong through the narrows under the rock of the old fortress city (the word *kebec* was Algonquin for "narrows"), around the lovely Ile d'Orléans into its firth with the flanking hills rising, finally, to the height and dignity of true mountains.

There are also the great tributaries, each with a multitude of stories and legends of its own. The Richelieu, draining Lake Champlain through the richest farming valley of Quebec, was also the invasion route for a century and a half of warfare until at last Gentlemanly Johnny Burgoyne marched down it from Montreal to suffer at Saratoga one of the most decisive defeats in the history of the world. There is the St. Francis, river of the Eastern Townships with their deep volcanic lakes and rolling hills like the Scottish Lowlands; the Ottawa, *la grande rivière* of the voyageurs; the wild St. Maurice down which the logs come, followed by the lumbermen roaring into Trois Rivières when the season's work is done; the Montmorency with its falls hanging against the cliff like a stained white scarf 265 feet high; finally the Saguenay, so deep and wide from Chicoutimi to Tadoussac it can hardly be called a river at all.

There is more to the physical St. Lawrence even than this. Only a few years back in geological time — little more than 10,000 years as a matter of fact — the St. Lawrence system was the vastest ever known. It drained much more than the middle-west of North America; it also drained much of the west. For when Lake Agassiz submerged most of the prairies on both sides of the present international border and covered with deep water an area almost as great as the Caspian Sea's, the St. Lawrence drained it as well as the Great Lakes, for Agassiz's waters used to spill over into Lake Superior.

Yet the St. Lawrence is more than a river, more even than a system of waters. It has made nations. It has been the moulder of the lives of millions — perhaps by now of hundreds of millions — in a multitude of different ways. At some point in my middle years, I realized that I myself belonged to the people whose lives the river has affected.

A few springs ago, standing by the greasy taffrail of a Manchester freighter drawing out from Quebec for its voyage down river to the sea, the idea came to me that my life would have been totally different had it not been for my association with this river. Though politically all my ancestors were in Canada long before Confederation, I am myself — if words mean anything — almost as much a New Canadian as any immigrant. A Nova Scotian from the Atlantic shore, I was all of twenty-eight years old before I came to live in the country my great-grandparents called "Canada".

Although the St. Lawrence forms the boundary between the United States and Canada all the way from Lake Ontario to Cornwall — the American negotiators in 1783 made sure they would control at least half of it — the river is as Canadian as the Rhine is German, and has profoundly affected the collective character of the people who live beside it.

I never understood this when first I came to Montreal. Canada — *Lower* Canada, as some old people in Nova Scotia still called it — had given me the job I could not find anywhere else in those depression years. I wanted to become a writer then, but I did not know how to write and I had to eat, so I taught school and wrote in my spare time. The life around me was stimulating and subtly different from any I had known anywhere else. The country I was living in was different, and so was its atmosphere. The most astonishing thing about the Canadians, it seemed to me, was their habit of never discussing so many of the things other people talk about. They took it for granted that everyone knew these things. They seemed to me the greatest takers-for-granted I had ever met in my life. Taking things for granted, I remember saying to one of them once, may well be the chief single characteristic of the Canadian people.

The English character we believe we know: it has been revealed in thousands of books in which Englishmen have defined and presented themselves. The American character, or at least what is now called the American Image, has been displayed on movie screens all over the world and in the pages of most of the magazines which Canadians read. But the Canadians, apparently, have no public image internationally recognized save the utterly false one of a frontier personality. I wanted to know them not only because I liked them, but because they puzzled me. Outwardly they were more disciplined even than the English – I had been at Oxford and had seen what the English can do when they get drunk and go wild. But these Laurentian people, at least in Montreal, could hold their liquor like judges, and yet they seemed to me tough right into their cores. Hockey was their great emotional outlet. It was their game and they had invented it, and those who say that hockey is tougher now than it used to be simply don't remember. They played the game tougher than the Irish play hurley, laconically smashing each other over the head with sticks and laconically submitting to several hundred stitches in the course of a normal professional career. Yet these same hockey players, with few exceptions, looked like quiet business men off the ice.

The Canadians did not boast as nearly everyone else does – as the Nova Scotians do, and the English also in their deceptive way. The boys I taught at school were not particularly good pupils, and on the whole were inferior in their work to the boys I had studied with at home. They never got into brawls. On the other hand, in the boxing competitions that occurred every spring, they beat each other up with a cold-blooded courage that seemed to me almost sinister, for hardly anyone ever took the trouble to learn how to box properly. They just went in there and hit because that was what they were expected to do, and when the bout was over they never talked about it, criticized it or even pretended to like boxing.

A baffling people they are because of this self-control which has been forced on them by the conditions of living here. They did not even seem aware they possessed it, yet often I have thought a Chinese would feel at home with some of these old Montreal families, whether the families speak English or French. A Frenchman told me once that he considered the women of the old Laurentian families to be the only truly mature women in North America; after some thirty years in the Province of Quebec, I think he was right.

But in no respect is this Lower Canadian control better displayed than in public and business life. It was, and perhaps still is, a life as corrupt as that of Walpole's England, yet they themselves are not apparently corrupted by it, though some of the political tools they employ certainly are. Their attitude toward corruption was the same as their attitude toward almost everything: since it was here, nobody could change it. Therefore it must be lived with. Why? I used to ask myself. Why this disconcerting maturity, this self-defeating tolerance, this feeling for quality combined with an unspoken conviction that quality lives on sufferance? Why this ingrained habit of dealing with the world behind a series of public masks which they, locally among themselves, always knew to be masks? Above all, why this modesty concerning themselves? For though Lower Canadians – and I am still speaking as a Nova Scotian – have infuriated their fellow nationals of all the other Canadian regions, and not a few Americans and English as well, by this bland assumption that their ways are unchangeable, thirty years of living among them have convinced me that modesty is their chief collective fault.

At first I saw them as a Scot or an Irishman coming to London sees the English, and they irritated me. They lacked our candour. I grudged having to admit that the Laurentian population was the core of the country to which my own province had belonged ever since 1867. I was angered (as a Scot is by the same behaviour among the English toward his own country), by their total indifference to the Maritimes and their easy sense of superiority toward the West. As for their feelings toward Toronto and Ontario, no matter how rich Toronto becomes, I will never live to see the day when a true Montrealer will bring himself to take Toronto seriously. Or rather – for the Laurentian people are masters at thinking on several different levels at once – they will take Toronto with total seriousness on the level on which Toronto takes herself, but at the same time will retain an inward smile, a feeling similar to what the English have when they think of the Americans.

But soon I found myself liking the Laurentian people, as most Scots like the English once they have lived for a time in London. Then I heard myself saying that Montreal was my home, and that I did not – indeed could not – live comfortably anywhere else for a long time. And it was about then, in search of my new-found self, that I began studying the lineaments of the so-called Canadian nation. Soon it appeared that the secret of their collective essence was intimately, profoundly, connected with the St. Lawrence River.

Now it so happened that I had seen many famous rivers before I ever visited the St. Lawrence. I had lived beside the Thames for several years. I had sailed on the Danube and the Rhine, had walked the bridges of the Seine, the Meuse and the Tiber, had travelled up the Hudson and Delaware and down the Mississippi. Once, admittedly, I had come up the St. Lawrence by steamer from England as far as Quebec, but Quebec, after all, is an ocean port. But now, living in Montreal and driving along the river-fronting roads, I saw the St. Lawrence in terms only of itself. This was no farmer's river; though there are some rich bottoms along the stream, the fertile valley is extremely narrow. But there was grandeur – grandeur of a kind I never saw on any river until, years later, I went to the Mackenzie. And I discovered, belatedly, that the fate of the St. Lawrence has been always to be an avenue to settlement elsewhere, to power and to empire.

Physically its impact is tremendous: it is as though nature here was a spendthrift. So much space, so much water, and so little of it useful. Trying to describe the St. Lawrence below Montreal in my novel *Two Solitudes* I wrote a *bravura* passage which still seems to me valid so far as it goes:

"Nowhere has nature wasted herself as she has done here. There is enough water in the St. Lawrence to irrigate half of Europe, but the river pours right out of the continent into the sea.

No amount of water can irrigate stones, and most of Quebec is solid rock. It is as though millions of years back in geologic time a sword had been plunged through the rock from the Atlantic to the Great Lakes and savagely wrenched out again, and the pure water of the continental reservoir, unmuddied and almost useless to farmers, drains untouchably away. In summer the clouds pass over it in soft, cumulus, pacific towers, endlessly forming and dissolving to make a welter of movement about the sun. In winter when there is no storm the sky is generally empty, blue and glittering over the ice and snow, and the sun stares out of it like a cyclops' eye."

An exaggeration, perhaps, but not too big a one. I went on to speak of the old Quebec farms hugging the shores between the rocky uplands and the stream; of the roads on either side of the river like a pair of village main streets linking the settlements, one street nearly a thousand miles long if you follow it down the Gaspé shore to the open waters of the Gulf. I wrote of the manner in which the land was divided in early days between seigneurs and their sons, then between tenants and their sons, with the result that sections of the lower river remind you of the course of a gigantic steeplechase, the fences making long rectangles as they run inland, the farms established in this long, narrow shape because a river frontage was vital in the days when the river was the chief means of communication. Finally I wrote of Montreal where the Canadian races meet without really mingling, the pulse of their encounter throbbing from east to west across the whole land.

As *Two Solitudes* was a novel of Quebec, I did not speak about the upper river. There, of course, the whole lie of the land is different. It is gentler, warmer and much more kind, nor is grey the predominant colour suggested by the environment. In summer the upper river is bluer, more gay and shining, younger looking and wonderfully kind to farmers.

But I was talking of the life the river has imposed on the Canadian people, and the character it has formed.

The St. Lawrence, as everyone knows, has been the most fought-over stream in the North American continent — much more so than the Mississippi, though no St. Lawrence battle, thank God, cost a fraction of the casualties of Vicksburg. Its present population has grown out of the very sediment of history. The original French who came over from Normandy and Brittany are French certainly. But they have been here so long, and the life of their ancestors has been so hard, that the character of French Canada is utterly different from that of metropolitan France. Heaven only knows how many of the Scottish soldiers who stormed Quebec in 1759 stayed in Canada and disappeared into the French-Canadian race, or how many Irish did likewise when they arrived in Quebec during the time of the potato famine. It would be interesting to know, but impossible to discover, what percentage of Celtic blood still runs in the veins of French Canadians answering to names like Polycarpe Fraser, Onesime O'Reilly or just plain Jean-Baptiste Tremblay. Is the famous fire of *les Canadiens* entirely derived from the dour stubbornness of Normandy? Or again, how many of the aboriginal inhabitants were Christianized, absorbed and changed?

But the St. Lawrence has woven together more racial strands than these, and with them the politics, the loyalties, the resentments and the habits to which the various racial groups were committed. The upper river received thousands of Loyalists after the American Revolution. Quebec, Montreal and Kingston for years harboured British garrisons. Scotch, English, Irish and American business and professional men, now joined by thousands of New Canadians from Europe, have lived side by side with the French in Montreal. After the fur trade began to fail – certainly after the North West Company fell to the Bay – hundreds of Americans came up to Montreal to do business and the influence of the Bank of Montreal, following the old course of the river into the interior, for years was dominant even in Chicago. The flotsam and jetsam of history, the ruins and recoveries of racial and religious hopes. The miracle is – and surely it *is* a miracle – that the nation built around the St. Lawrence has turned out to be one of the most stable in the world.

For this fact we may thank the character and habits of the Laurentian people, whether of French, English, Scottish, or Irish origins, whether of the upper or the lower river. "Intricate" is the word which fits best its collective pattern. As I have come to know this region, I find myself running out of adjectives in an attempt to describe its people so that others will know what they are like. Does it make any sense to say that a Canadian – not a Maritimer, not anyone west of Kingston – is apt to be a person so subtle that compared to him the average Englishman is an open book? Does it make any sense to say this while admitting that he is not

intellectual, and that he seldom takes intellectuals seriously
enough to become angry with them? But complex this man is in
a sense so profound it can almost be called instinctual. Not even
if he wished, could he afford to be whole-heartedly one thing or
the other. To take both cash and credit – among the English-
speaking Laurentians it has generally been considered safer to
make sure of the cash and let the credit go. To be profoundly
Catholic yet at the same time openly anti-clerical – among edu-
cated French Canadians this balancing act has become automatic.
In England I have often felt provincial, but seldom naïve. In
Montreal I have never felt provincial, but naïve about once a
week as I literally *hear* the things that are never uttered. They
build the fences high around their racial and political compounds,
and they sally out from them armed with a curious courtesy. No
matter what the intensity of their private feelings, English- and
French-speaking Laurentians never utter deliberately a hostile
word against the other's group in the presence of a person belong-
ing to it, and if they do so by accident, they feel ashamed for
having let their standards down.

Douglas Le Pan once described the voyageur as "Hamlet with
the countenance of Horatio", and Robertson Davies remarked that
nobody had ever compressed into a single phrase more insight
into the Canadian character. The phrase applies perfectly to the
greatest statesman ever produced in the Laurentian region. One
could almost say that Sir John A. Macdonald's entire career was
the result of Laurentian tensions and needs. His whole life was
one of Hamletian doubt and imagination, of Horatian self-control
and endurance. Circumstances always compelled him to achieve
his results without dramatizing them. I think of Macdonald at the
Washington Conference of 1871, where neither the English nor
the American delegates took him seriously because he was a
colonial. All his life he had been forced to deal in a calculus of
politics, and he did so then. He cared, but he did not let them
know how much he cared, when his pride was insulted and his
country scorned. He probably knew it would be like this when he
went to Washington determined that Canada remain in the
British Empire whether the British wanted her or not, determined
also that the British garrisons should leave the forts along the St.
Lawrence if their departure would result in a demilitarization of
the frontier. To serve the interests *both* of Britain and the United
States was the only way in which Canada could hope to become

independent. If the others did not understand this, Sir John had always understood it, and he came home with what he wanted — with the cash, but not with the international credit.

As a Nova Scotian I find it impossible to believe that Macdonald could ever have succeeded in Canada — or rather, *with* Canada — had he been as dramatic and outspoken as our own Joseph Howe. In Nova Scotia we had never felt any special need to bank down our native fires. The Royal Navy with its base in Halifax sheltered us; our pride was a British pride. But in Laurentia this could never be so because the country was a pocket in the continent's heart. The United States literally touched it; within it, the opposite prides of French and English living together in the same towns and sharing the government and the river strained against each other. Again and again these Laurentian minorities have longed to shout aloud that they hate one another, but almost always they bite their tongues. And then, taking a second thought, they realize that what they hate is not one another but the frustrations resulting from the necessity of living an eternal compromise. So it has come about that the Laurentian people, over the years, have acquired the art of looking at life with a sextuple vision — as individuals, as members of their own racial or religious group, as Canadian citizens, as North Americans always required to balance their own interests in a kind of invisible juggling act with their southern neighbours whom they deeply like, as cultural scions of the French and English archetypes, and finally as cold-headed realists in an international society.

"If we could only get ourselves included in a genuine western alliance, or even a genuine state, then, in the multiplicity of nations involved, we might be able to hold our own against our friends (i.e. the Americans) a little better. As it is, locked up in the same house with them, we are almost necessarily their prisoners."

These words reached me in a brief, casual letter from an elderly and distinguished Canadian historian. "Locked up in the same house with our friends" — the Laurentians have always felt like that, and therefore they are supreme realists — the river has made them so — in a world in which all nations, friends and enemies alike, will soon be compelled to realize that to be locked up with one another has become the modern human condition. No wonder that the needs of Laurentian life produced the fantastic political realism which resulted in the concept of the self-governing dominion under the Crown, and later in the nebulous solidity of the concept of the Commonwealth.

The freighter felt the tug of the current flowing through the gorge between Quebec and Lévis, and looking around I felt the excitement this famous scene always gives me. The sky over the purple-grey city was turbulent, and the distant mountains were streaked with patches of brightness as the sun struck through clouds. Here, as everywhere in the central and lower St. Lawrence, was visible the perpetual Canadian frontier, the rocky hills of the Shield.

Travelling along the St. Lawrence aboard a working freighter is still the best way to know this river. On the upper reaches where the Seaway now runs it can be very intimate, the ocean-going ships sailing through farms and villages. Once years ago, before the Seaway was built, stealing past the little Ontario town of Cardinal, I seemed to be looking into everyone's home. We slipped noiselessly along in the dark virtually between the United States and Canada, and I will never forget the startling beauty of a lighted window behind which a young girl, smiling secretly to herself, was brushing her hair. Nor again another night in 1940, the month that France fell, the feeling of hope and security when I looked across that river-frontier to the lights shining in the most powerful country in the world. Standing now on the freighter below the pile of Quebec City, I wondered how anyone could believe that a nation containing a city like this is really young at heart.

Quebec, to me at least, has the air of a city that never was young. No community in America, few in Europe, give out such a feeling of intense, rain-washed antiquity. A little like Calais, perhaps, but far nobler on its rock with the wilderness behind it and the great river at its foot. Those stern grey walls with their Norman and Mediterranean roofs two centuries ago sheltered an embattled, isolated people who lived as long and as hard in a decade as most communities live in a century. Even their religion contributed to their tensions, for the Quebec of Bishop Laval was a product of the fierce intolerance of the Counter Reformation, in turn a riposte to the equally fierce intolerance of Protestantism.

I looked up at the palisade of the Citadel polished smoothly grey by wind, rain, snow and ice with the river sheer below it, and remembered an evening not long before when I had stood on the grass of the King's Bastion beside a famous English statesman with whom we had been playing croquet. A corporal's guard had marched round the corner of the blockhouse to the flagstaff. Wind tossed the clouds and across the river rain was falling on Lévis. The soldiers were guardsmen in red coats and bearskins, and as the flag came down one of them sounded the British Last Post over the river whence, two centuries ago, British shells had whirred into the Lower Town and smashed it to a shambles. I saw tears in the eyes of the English statesman and heard him murmur:

"If Winston could see this, he'd talk of it for hours."

Our host said with a quiet smile: "If he knew those guardsmen spoke French, I fancy he might talk about it half the night."

But Quebec, as everyone knows who has ever lived in it as long as a week, is no monument. The noble convent of the Ursulines looks as it always did; the belfry bells seem to ring incessantly; the black soutanes of the priests flap in the wind round the corners. But the Plouffe Family lives here along with their furiously energetic creator. Maurice Duplessis ruled here for years with a personal authority which almost, but never quite, verged on a dictatorship. Here also the statesmen, generals, admirals and airmen of the Western Alliance met to set their seals to the master plan which won the Second World War. And here, in this so-called monument of the past, Albert Guay conceived and executed the most thoroughly modern murder of the twentieth century.

The ship turned into the channel leading round the southern tip of the Ile d'Orléans, the sun broke through the clouds and slowly set, and I found myself recalling Conrad's chapter at the opening of *Heart of Darkness*. Conrad's scene was a river even more famous, the Thames, but the thoughts it evoked in the novelist seemed to fit the St. Lawrence better than any of my own:

"The old river rested in its broad reach unruffled at the decline of day, after ages of good service to the race that people its banks, spread out in tranquil dignity to a waterway leading to the uttermost parts of the earth."

Ages of good service! At least three centuries of varied service the St. Lawrence has given, and not the least of its gifts has been the knowledge the problems it created have taught the people who have been involved in its story. The chief lesson of all is that history is invariably ironical, that the greatest men of action seldom understand the true meaning of what they do, that the results that flow from their lives are seldom as they planned them.

Irony has been connected with the St. Lawrence from the very beginning.

Jacques Cartier seems to have been as practical a mariner as ever sailed from a Brittany port, but when he entered that enormous estuary in 1534, when he sailed on and on up the firth, what else could he have assumed than that the St. Lawrence was the Northwest Passage? What importance he attached to the wild grapes he found in abundance on the Ile d'Orléans! Was he disappointed, or was he stricken with awe when he stood on Mount Royal after his ship had been halted by the rapids and stared into the unpeopled land into which the great river disappeared? And why did his own government, when he returned with the news of his discovery, do nothing about it for nearly a full century? Had France moved promptly then, the whole of North America would have been hers.

Irony has haunted most of the great lives connected with the St. Lawrence. LaSalle, seeing the rapids boiling past his seigneury on the southern shore of Montreal Island, may not have been as naïve as the jokers who called the rapids "Lachine" in mockery of his dream, but China seems to have been his dream-goal when he paddled and portaged all the way to the delta of the Mississippi. The meaning of the river's future was clearly closed to Jean Talon, or at least to the French government who employed him, when he established along its banks a replica of a European feudal system. Was it not in America that the first decisive blow against the old privileged classes was struck? Laurentian facts quite baffled Laval's dream of a Catholic-American empire with a cross on every hill from the Gaspé to the Gulf of Mexico. The same river which led the French canoes into the interior also invited the Royal Navy in behind them, and at Quebec the French were trapped.

Irony also haunted the Europeans who thought about the St. Lawrence. The cleverest man in the eighteenth century is remembered in Canada chiefly for one epigram which is repeated only to make a fool of him, namely that along the St. Lawrence two empires were fighting for a few acres of snow.

But what of the English conquerors of Quebec — what did their victory on the St. Lawrence achieve for *them*? The English experience with the river was the most exquisitely ironical of all.

In the middle eighteenth century when Lord Chatham studied his maps in London, it seemed very clear to him that if Britain could become master of the St. Lawrence, the whole of North

America would be hers permanently. The river was the sole avenue into the Ohio Territory from which the English of the Thirteen Colonies were barred by the Appalachians. Imperial France was in a bad condition internally with a corrupt government, a weak navy and a worthless king. So Pitt made his decision and mounted the greatest overseas armada in the history of Europe up to that time. Louisbourg fell and the American auxiliary troops razed it. The St. Lawrence was open, no longer did a French fortress lie across the British lines of communication, and the French at Quebec were cut off from a discouraged and (for the moment) decadent motherland. Whether or not Wolfe would have preferred to be the author of a minor poem than to have taken Quebec is a matter in some dispute. He certainly took Quebec, and four years later the government of France ceded Canada to England.

This was the most fatal victory England ever won. For now that the Laurentian threat was removed, the American revolutionary movement grew rapidly. When the Quebec Act, the most liberal document ever granted to a conquered people up to that time, came into effect in 1775, it fired the mine in the southern colonies. The French Canadians had been the enemies of the British Americans for a century and a half. The French Canadians were as militantly Catholic as the Americans were militantly dissenting Protestants. The Revolutionary War broke out and the Americans, as everyone knows, won it.

So came about the greatest irony of all: at the end of the war the chief North American region flying the British flag was Laurentia, the home of Britain's ancient enemy. And as a component part of *that* irony, the Protestant United Empire Loyalists, ousted from their American homes, now had to trek north to build in the wilderness along the upper river, and from then on were doomed to share the river with a people they had always accounted their enemies. Their foolish attempts to dominate the French in the next century and a half served only to make their own lot more difficult. For the French waited. The endless patience enforced upon them enabled them to wait and wait until now, in the mid-twentieth century, Quebec is theirs. It was said in ancient times: "Greece, captive, led captive her captors." The French Canadians have been too shrewd to say as much in public, but they say it in private many times, and so they should. By waiting, by enduring, by yielding again and again on small issues but never on a vital one, they have seen their concept of a dual culture accepted by the English-speaking compatriots whose ancestors considered them a conquered people.

An imperial river – the St. Lawrence has always been that. After the first commercial empire of the St. Lawrence withered, the empire of timber took its place. Then came the railway empire, and soon the prairies discovered by the voyageurs became virtual provinces of the Laurentian cities, their tribute manifest in the Victorian castles which still survive on the southern slopes of Mount Royal. With the coming of hydro-electricity, empire moved from the railway barons and the forest industries to the manufacturers. Now the power bred out of the St. Lawrence system has changed in a few decades the whole nature of traditional French-Canadian life, turning an erstwhile race of simple folk into one of the most highly organized industrial communities on the continent, with results to their character as yet unpredictable.

Finally, with the opening of the International Seaway, the rapids were conquered and ocean-going ships of more than 20,000 tons began moving into the continent's heart. The Power Project connected with the Seaway is sure to create still another Laurentian empire along the former agricultural reaches of the upper river. What course this one will take I would not presume to guess; there have been enough bad guesses connected with the St. Lawrence as it is. But already it seems certain that the St. Lawrence, breeder of nations though she has been, will never tolerate a narrow nationalism in North America. Just as the French and English have had to sink their differences in order to share the river, so now, more closely than ever, Canada and the United States are permanently tied together by the river which theoretically divides them.

Yet the St. Lawrence has changed its appearance very little over the years. The lower Thames is overwhelmed by London, the lower Hudson is utterly dominated by the towers of Manhattan, the Elbe disappears into Hamburg. But when you fly out of Dorval on the London or Halifax plane, the river below you is so enormous that even the seaway excavations look no more than a trivial scar along the south bend of Laprairie Basin. At night Montreal is a scintillating wash of coloured lights pouring in a sluice of brightness down the long slope of the mountain to the stream. But in a matter of minutes you leave it behind. The river is still too big to be dominated in its landscape by anything human connected with it. Below Quebec there are long reaches which look exactly as they did to Cartier. Even along the upper river, even in the section of the old International Rapids where the engineering work connected with the Seaway and Power Project has been most spectacular, the changes wrought in the landscape are still relatively small compared to the landscape's vastness.

My freighter turned into the channel round the Ile d'Orléans and an incoming ship broke out her lights. We passed her and went on into the gathering darkness of the stream. After dinner I came out on deck and began counting the ships we passed, but as I could see nothing but their lights I could only guess at their nationalities. For hours I walked around the decks looking at the lights of the old parishes slipping by, and leaning over the side I could hear the hiss of brine along the plates of the ship. The water was almost entirely salt now, but we were still many miles inland from Father Point. I went to bed and slept eight hours, and in the morning we were still in what the maps call the river. A school of white porpoises flashed about us very close and a deck-hand told me they were unique to this region. A steward contradicted him and said they can also be found in the estuary of the River Plate and probably he was right, for he was torpedoed there in the war. We passed Anticosti and entered the Gulf, but we were still, in a sense, within the St. Lawrence system as we passed slowly north along the flank of Labrador where yet another empire connected with the St. Lawrence is a-building. Newfoundland appeared on the starboard bow as I was going to bed. The next morning broke cold and foggy, I dressed and saw the icebergs in the Strait of Belle Isle. Some time in the forenoon we rounded Cape Bon and were out of the St. Lawrence system at last.

Ten days later, after coming down from Manchester in an English June, I found myself in London again after many years. Alone and caught by a bus strike, I spent hours of every day walking the famous old streets. As a young man in Nova Scotia I had not looked west but east, and London had been the first great city I had seen. Now I found myself looking at London with fresh eyes, and because I have moved about a good deal in my life, I began asking myself if there was any city I knew remotely like it. There is only one London, of course, and it still is the greatest city on earth; in time it will probably become as eternal as Rome. But I noticed one thing about myself in connection with London I had never felt before. I felt at home. I was prepared now for its scope and attitude. One evening walking down the Haymarket toward Trafalgar Square I remembered an essay about London by V. S. Pritchett, the one in which he said that the word evoked in his mind by the image of Rome was "murder", the word by the image of Paris "feminine", but the word brought forth to fit London was "experience".

I had it then. "Experience", above all other words in the language, is the one which seems to me to fit the city of Montreal where I live now. It still is, and always will be, the commercial capital of the St. Lawrence. Its character has been formed by the river which made its existence possible and its importance inevitable.

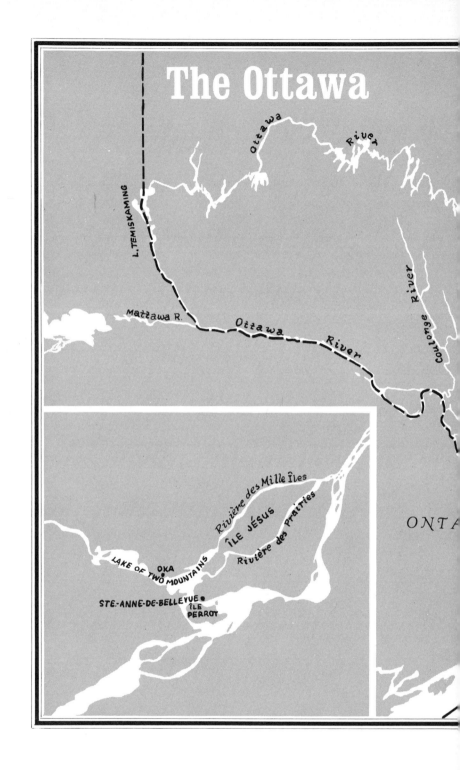

The Ottawa

Ottawa River

Coulonge River

L. TEMISKAMING

Mattawa R.

Ottawa River

Rivière des Mille Îles

ÎLE JÉSUS

Rivière des Prairies

LAKE OF TWO MOUNTAINS

OKA

ONTA

STE-ANNE-DE-BELLEVUE

ÎLE PERROT

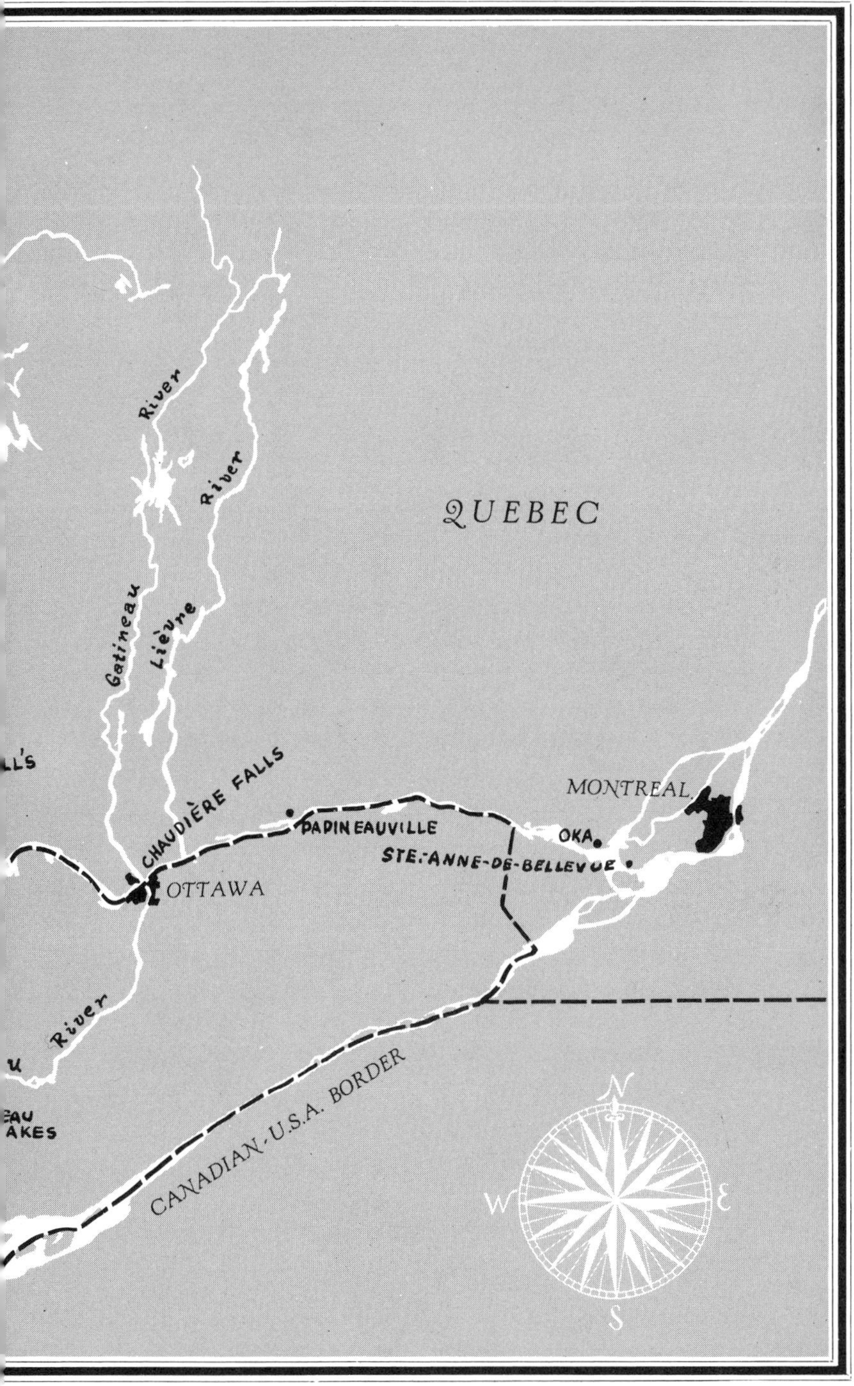

QUEBEC
Gatineau River
Lièvre River
CHAUDIÈRE FALLS
PAPINEAUVILLE
MONTREAL
OKA
STE.-ANNE-DE-BELLEVUE
OTTAWA
River
CANADIAN-U.S.A. BORDER
N
W
E
S

The Ottawa

An autumn ago I was strolling on the embankment above the Ottawa River just below the point where the stream enters the Lake of Two Mountains. A cold wind was mournful in the pine grove, and I remembered how different everything had been the first time I had seen this grove. I was in the company of the same old gentleman I was with now, but it had been twenty years ago and summer. Everything had been delicious: a lace of foam was visible where a light breeze blew against the current, a lace of shadows lay on the pine needle floor of the grove. But our hearts were cold that day because France had just fallen. Everything in that summer of 1940 was so lovely except the one thing we thought about.

Now on this autumn afternoon of cold winds and grey skies the region had the grim look of early November in Canada without sun. But our hearts were light then. The old gentleman, no older in spirit now than he had been twenty years before, but with twenty more years of distinguished service behind him — two ambassadorships and one high commissionership — had just learned from Oxford that his translation of Dante's *Inferno* had been accepted with enthusiasm. He had always written poetry as a hobby. Now in his retirement he had completed the finest translation of the *Inferno* I had ever read.

He chuckled. "The publishers insist that I do the *Purgatorio* for them. In fairness I had to warn them that there is every likelihood that I will arrive there in person before I finish it."

He asked me what I was writing now, and I told him I had been spending the last two years trying to turn myself into a river. Trying to *feel* like a river, even; now I was trying to feel like the Ottawa.

He had lived in this place near the Trappist monastery at Oka every summer of his life for nearly forty years. As he was studious in all things, I assumed that he knew much more about the Ottawa than I would ever learn. In front of his property, he told me, he had water rights extending far into the lake, and with a charming smile he said it was very pleasant to own a part of a river like this.

"But of course," he added, "this is the unknown river of Canada."

"That much I've already discovered."

Though I had lived in Montreal for a full generation, had crossed bridges over the Ottawa so often I could not count the times, and had even worked one summer in the capital, I had taken the river for granted as everyone else seems to do. The old question about its length was revealing only in so far as it underlined everyone's ignorance about the river itself. I had been asking people how long they thought the Ottawa was, and one man gave a length of a hundred miles, another of two hundred and a third went so far as to say it would not surprise him if it was as long as two hundred and fifty. I remarked that the Ottawa's chief tributary, the Gatineau, was nearly as long as that, and he looked at me in mild surprise. "Is it?" he said.

My friend smiled: "That's so typical. Somehow or other the Ottawa got lost when the St. Lawrence took its place. But it's a river full of character. It's most unusual, you know. And it's much senior to the St. Lawrence. But then, I suppose you've found that out for yourself."

It so happened that I had found it out, but only a few days previously. A geographer I know had told me that the St. Lawrence was a geographical afterthought. Once upon a time it was the Ottawa, not the St. Lawrence, which had drained the Great Lakes. Its channel had been the old voyageurs' route through French River, Lake Nipissing and the Mattawa, and it discharged an immense volume of water into the channel now claimed by the St. Lawrence below Montreal. But changes had occurred in the contours of the land, there had been an upthrust of the earth and the lake water had found itself the new channel which now is the upper St. Lawrence. It is significant that there are no northern tributaries of the St. Lawrence above the point where the Ottawa now enters it. The little Rideau River, together with its lakes, is really a kind of water bridge between the Ottawa and the St. Lawrence, for though it tumbles over its cliff into the Ottawa, its flow is very gentle and at the southern end there is a still stretch on the Rideau which receives water from the bay just below the point where the St. Lawrence channel drains out of Lake Ontario.

Today, of course, the Ottawa is regarded as the chief tributary of the St. Lawrence system. Yet *la grande rivière*, which once was itself the master stream of a great system, has retained a genuine air of independence. It also possesses, as my friend had said, some features very unusual, and its own northern tributaries come through wild country.

Years ago my brother-in-law paddled down one of these, the Lièvre, which is the Ottawa's second longest tributary now. Locally the Lièvre is pronounced in French as "Lever" because, after its original discovery and naming by French explorers, nothing was done with it until some Scotch people came to it after the Conquest. The Scotch mispronounced the French name, and when French Canadians moved in later, they accepted the mispronunciation. The Ottawa story is charged with anomalies like this and with forgotten episodes. However, this canoe trip down the Lièvre was one of the most vivid recollections of my brother-in-law's life. In places the Lièvre is very dangerous with fierce rapids, and for long stretches it runs through a forest as lonely as it was in the days when the hunter Algonquins roamed it. My brother-in-law had studied the contours of the Ottawa system, and he gave me what I believe is the only sensible answer I have received concerning its length.

"I don't think anyone knows how long the Ottawa is," he said.

If I talk about the Ottawa's length now it is only as a means of describing the character of a stream more unusually constituted than any I have studied. Usually the river's source is given as the head of Lake Temiskaming, and the distance from there to the Sainte-Anne-de-Bellevue Passage is roughly 696 miles. But what lies behind Lake Temiskaming? At least one official Quebec map shows the thread of the *Rivière Outaouais* winding far back into Quebec toward the north-*east*, deep into the Laurentian forest through a chain of weirdly shaped lakes all the way to Lac au Bouleau in the LaVérendrye National Park.

As no single lake can be described as the original source of a river which flows through a long series of lakes, and is fed by most of them, it is therefore quite impossible to determine how long the Ottawa is. But these lakes give the Ottawa its uniquely repetitive character. The river usually enters each lake with a mild current, and with the pressure of the lake behind it, discharges into the ensuing channel in a short, heavy rush. That is why there were eighteen portages on the Ottawa between Lake of Two Mountains and the mouth of the Mattawa, and why the journey up the Grand

River was such a hard one for the canoe parties.

The voyageurs estimated the Long Sault at three leagues — in other words, at about six miles — and they made it in three portages. Though some of the bolder men tried to shoot the rapids coming down stream, this was very dangerous. John Macdonell, on his voyage up the Ottawa in the spring of 1793, noted a cross on one of these portages marking the grave of a young Christian Indian who had been drowned while trying to save time by shooting the rapids in his canoe. He also reports that several canoes of his own brigade of expert commercial voyageurs were damaged on the river and that the work of portaging was very hard. The carrying place about the Chaudière Falls was a troublesome one. The longest on the river was called LaMontagne; a mile long, it was also very steep. Macdonell says it took his party twenty-four hours to clear it. But the rushes of swift water out of the lakes are generally quite short. The one at the Allumettes, for instance, was measured at fifteen to twenty paces only, and in the slack waters of the lakes paddling was easy and rapid, especially if a wind was behind the canoes. But though the voyageurs wore the carrying places smooth between Sainte-Anne-de-Bellevue and the Mattawa, the Ottawa above this point was virtually left alone in the fur-trading days. It is little visited now except by people in the lumber business.

Still less familiar are some of the eleven tributaries. Everyone living in Ottawa City knows the lower Gatineau, and everyone knows the Rideau. But one of the most interesting of the tributaries, it seems to me, is the Coulonge. It is 135 miles long and flows south for all of its course. But if you trace it to its origin, what do you find? You find the Coulonge issuing from a section of LaVérendrye National Park where the water pattern is so intricate that you can almost persuade yourself that the Coulonge draws some of its source waters from the same swampy Lac au Bouleau which is often considered the prime source of the Ottawa itself. It would be pleasant to imagine that it does, for then one could argue that for most of its source the Ottawa flows in a circle, and that the final stretch from the mouth of the Coulonge in Campbell's Bay is merely the tail of a vast, fluvial Q. But enough of these paradoxes. Think of the Ottawa as a chain of elongated lakes with a current connecting them and flowing through them and you have the general character of the river as a geological agent.

In a wider sense I think of the Ottawa as a complex of contrasts, all of them inherent in the pattern of the Canadian nation and the Canadian land.

Most of the lakes on the central and lower Ottawa are gentle with reeds through which the water sighs and among which hundreds of thousands of wild duck breed. Were it not for the rapids the lakes would make navigation from Montreal as easy as it is on the St. Lawrence, and plans have been considered for the construction of an Ottawa Seaway. One of these days they will probably be realized. But now we have the tranquil lakes succeeded by the quick gush of rapids at the end of them, and this is the first of the contrasts.

The next one, it seems to me, is the difference between the north and the south bank. The Ottawa forms the boundary between Ontario and Quebec all the way from Lake Temiskaming to the confluence with the St. Lawrence, and for much of the distance the contrast between the two terrains is absolute and visible. Southward in Ontario are rich farms and rolling hills, with a wealth of hardwood trees. But the moment you cross the river and enter Quebec, you are in the rocky Laurentian highlands among the conifers, and the land is so useless to farms it has remained just about as wild as it always was.

"Do you mean there are *wolves* here?" I asked a man on Allumette Island a few springs ago.

He had been asked the question before, and in the same tone of voice.

"Over there" — and he pointed to the high bush country, "there are so many wolves that I don't like going far into those woods without a rifle. Let me tell you a story about our wolves."

I was sceptical, having heard the remark attributed to an editor at Sault-Sainte-Marie that he had yet to meet a man who had been eaten by a wolf, but this man looked solid and responsible. He was an American, a professional hunter and guide, and he had come here years ago from Pennsylvania because he had always liked wild country.

"Only last year," he said, "*in August*, I drove a tractor up there to take out a fishing party. In there among the hills a few miles, some Americans were fishing a lake. The fish were biting and on toward twilight the party didn't want to leave. I told them they'd better get moving on account of the wolves and they laughed at me. 'Wolves up here?' one of them said. 'Wolves in August? Wolves within a hundred and twenty-five miles of Ottawa City?'

"Well, I did a very foolish thing. I knew the deer had been taking a bad beating from the wolves lately because a few nights before some wolves had crossed the river and killed cattle on farms on the south side. That meant they were getting pretty hungry, for a wolf has to be desperate to enter a lighted country after dark. But anyhow, I went over to a birch tree and cut off a strip of bark and made myself a moose call. 'Listen and see what happens,' I said, and I began calling. Almost right away I heard a wolf howl. The howl was answered and I felt like the whole mountain was coming alive. 'Let's get out of here,' I said. 'Let's get out of here fast. I've only got three cartridges to my rifle.'

"So we got aboard the tractor — I had a trailer attached with some hay in it — and went down that trail as fast as she would move, which was only about thirty miles an hour. The tractor had no light and the trail was rough. There are hundreds of trails like that on the other side of the river leading to abandoned lumber camps. Pretty soon the wolves came out of the trees and began following. Then some more came in from the sides. It was like being hunted in a war, the way they came they seemed so organized. I don't mind saying I took them more seriously than my party did. How many there were I don't know, but there were enough to have torn us to pieces. They were closing in. They were getting confident when we came round a bend in the trail and there was a light in an Indian's cabin. I figure that light saved us, for they faded out."

I murmured something about not knowing the country was so wild.

The man smiled: "Across there it's just about as wild as it can get in Canada. The lumbermen haven't been working there for years, and their old bunkhouses make pretty good lairs. Once I found some wolf cubs in the ruins of an old bunkhouse and began playing with them and the next thing I saw was a pair of lobos staring at me."

I had heard the word "lobo" before, but not in Canada. In the States, lobo used to be the name for a solitary wolf, a smart wolf that preyed on cattle. The name is still used in states which have wolves.

"If I hadn't had my rifle," the man said, "I wouldn't be talking to you now."

This story I relate just as it was told to me, and to the best of my knowledge it is true. But a hundred miles lower down on the

Ottawa, nobody thinks about wolves.

The contrast between the settled and the wild — so typical of many parts of Canada — yields to a pattern of contrasts even more complex in the capital itself. There almost every influence in the country is visible and many of them are at odds with one another. Perhaps within twenty-five years' time the nation's capital will have become the beautiful, ordered thing the National Capital Planning Commission intends, but today its mixture of rawness and dignity reminds one of pictures of Washington at the time of the Civil War, except that the contrasts are all Canadian.

Parliament Hill stands nobly on its bluff with the foam-flecked river swirling below out of the Chaudière toward the mouth of the Gatineau and the Rideau Falls. Here, miraculously captured by the architects, are visibly united the three separate heritages which originally formed the nation. Nobody can look at Parliament Hill, especially in the evening from the little park behind the Château Laurier, without being reminded of ancient France, of West-minster and of Edinburgh Castle. Yet that splendid composition stands isolated in the commonplace red brick of old Bytown, and faces across the river not only to the Laurentian wilds, but also to one of the biggest lumber stacks in the country. The last time I was in Ottawa there shone at night, on top of that hideous indus-trial congeries in Hull, in brilliant Neon, a huge advertisement for toilet paper.

The Ottawa is not easy to picture, is almost impossible to define, and nowhere is its pattern more complex than at its end. Just before the confluence with the St. Lawrence, the river swells into the last and most beautiful of its many lakes. But out of Lake of Two Mountains, Ottawa water gushes into the St. Lawrence not by one channel but by four. On the south it flows around Ile Perrot through gaps at Dorion and Sainte-Anne-de-Bellevue, and this was the route of the old voyageurs. But the bulk of its water goes north-about and enters the St. Lawrence below Montreal. This archipelago is not a true delta, though sediment brought down by the river has certainly made its contribution to the rich topsoil of some of these islands.

At this point the map is further confused because the Ottawa (like the Rhine and the Yangtse) emerges under an entirely new set of names. The channel separating the mainland from the northern flank of Ile Jésus (the second largest island in the Mont-real archipelago) is called Rivière des Mille Iles; as the name implies, it is a rusty-brown stream sucking along through a welter of tiny islets. The other channel dividing Ile Jésus from Montreal Island is marked on the maps as Rivière des Prairies, but English-speaking Montrealers have further confused things by calling it "the Back River". Re-uniting, these two channels again become "the Ottawa", and after embracing the little Bout de l'Ile, the river finally merges with the St. Lawrence. But it does not lose itself. The Ottawa's amber hue — product not of mud but of root stain and iron stain — colours the main stream all the way down to Quebec and beyond, until finally the waters of the entire Laurentian system blend with the tides in the great firth below the Ile d'Orléans.

Before Queen Victoria selected Bytown as the capital of the Dominion of Canada, the Ottawa River served this continent, and also the French and British Empires, in several distinctly different ways. Its role as an avenue of exploration and trade has already been discussed. But even before the fur trade died out, the river became the centre of one of the world's largest lumbering industries. The south side of the valley, with its rolling land and good soil, offered a homeland to large contingents of settlers, most of them United Empire Loyalists and retired officers on half-pay, and over the years their quiet labour has helped to make Ontario our richest province.

The constructive influence of Americans on Canada has been profound from the day of Peter Pond to the age of Clarence Decatur Howe. So it was along the Ottawa. The creator of a farming and industrial society along *la grande rivière* of the voyageurs was neither a French Canadian nor a Scot of the North West Company; he was the Massachusetts Yankee, Philemon Wright.

Wright first visited the Ottawa in the last year of the eighteenth century, liked what he saw, and returned with a small colony to break land. But this man was destined for a career larger than farming. Wright possessed the Yankee talent for complex organization which sees one activity dovetailing into a dozen others. He was a surveyor, a farmer, a woodsman, a lumber man, and in the end he was a shipping and financial tycoon deeply involved in international affairs. Nor was anyone in Canadian history luckier in the coincidence of his private dream with a pressing public need.

When Wright surveyed the Ottawa forests he found an abundance of white pine standing two hundred feet tall — useless if nobody wanted them, a fortune if anyone did. Here also were oaks, hickories, maples, butternuts and cedars, and a strong, broad river flowed through them. Wright dreamed of "a fleet of a thousand ships carrying Ottawa timber to the sea", and with this end in mind, he conducted the first systematic survey of the river. The voyageurs had never done this because they had not found it necessary, and their maps were less adequate than most Montrealers believed. In Montreal, Wright was told that he could never succeed in driving logs economically. Heavy ships could not pass the Long Sault, and log rafts could not be conveyed through the Sainte-Anne-de-Bellevue Passage or controlled in rapids as violent as the Lachine. But Wright searched elsewhere, and found what he wanted in the north-about route past Bout de l'Ile which the voyageurs had neglected.

At this very time, and for the first time in history, the demand for Canadian lumber became exorbitant. Napoleon had countered the British naval blockade by imposing the Berlin Decrees which forbade the use of all continental ports to British ships. The Royal Navy, controlling the high seas, was able to convoy to England all necessary supplies but timber. For this they had depended for years on the Baltic ports of the Scandinavian countries. The very existence of the fleets — both naval and mercantile marine — depended on timber and the Admiralty became alarmed. In 1801 Nelson fought the Battle of Copenhagen to prevent the French from seizing the Danish fleet. In 1807, the British seized the remnants of the Danish fleet and held them as hostages. But still their shipyards were denied the use of Scandinavian timber.

Philemon Wright knew this well, and it was in that very year that his first shipment of Ottawa timber reached Quebec and was transferred to ocean-going vessels which carried it to England.

This was the beginning of a huge lumber industry which transformed the Ottawa Valley and made Quebec City the chief lumber port of the world. There was an old sea shanty sung in British, American and Canadian ships through much of the last century:

> *Have you ever been in Quebec*
> *Piling timber on the deck?*

Great fortunes were made in Ottawa timber over a period of a century and a half, and in modern times the industry has expanded to include pulp and paper, so that you cannot travel far along the Ottawa without smelling sulphur or seeing the tell-tale plume of yellow smoke that marks a pulp and paper factory.

But lumbering, though not so nomadic as fur-trading, by its very nature is bound to keep a human community frozen almost indefinitely in a state of cultural infancy. The lumbermen of the Ottawa cut over a territory and moved on, leaving the cut-over land until a new generation of trees grew up in sufficient quantity to make it profitable once more to destroy them. This meant that the lumbermen built nothing for permanence. Their communities were not towns but work camps, their buildings were not houses, but structures almost as temporary as the shacks they nailed down on the huge rafts they kept sending down the rivers. Nor were the men engaged in lumbering in the early days the kind who would ever build a cultivated society. They spent their lives in forest slums, and most of them were illiterate.

In the heyday of the lumbering business in the last century, the Ottawa was one of the toughest regions of North America; at times, one might think, almost as bad as in the days when the Iroquois war parties hunted the Algonquins and Dollard Des Ormeaux conducted his famous defence at the Long Sault, for there was a feeling of basic hopelessness among most proletariats in the last century. Until very recently the poor and uneducated – the people described in the Statue of Liberty's inscription as "the wretched refuse of your crowded shores" – performed most of the work now done by machinery, and were treated as such. Considered as economic units, machines were all they were. The work gangs along the Ottawa were almost the size of regiments, and matters were made worse by the practice of recruiting them racially, whether because the men preferred to work with their own kind, or because their employers instinctively followed the old principle of divide and rule. The hardness of their lives, the quality of their food, their isolation from normal society, the absence of family life, the feeling that they were spending their strength for an old age of poverty and loneliness – all these things combined to make them permanently quarrelsome. The Irish fought with the French, and feuds between shanties and shantymen endured for years while the character of the lumbermen remained the same. Generation after generation along the river they cut the trees, drove the logs, cleared them from jams, took them over waterfalls, and subsisted on a diet that exposed them to scurvy and boils: pea soup, pork and beans, scouse if they were lucky and gallons of tea the strength of lye.

It was directly out of this background that the present capital of Canada developed, and whenever I see the civil servants walking down Wellington Street with their brief cases, I marvel at the human capacity for rapid change.

For old Bytown, even old Ottawa, was a barbarous place. In 1832, when Colonel By and his Royal Engineers had completed their six-year job of digging (with the help of Irish labourers) the Rideau Canal with its forty-seven locks, the town named after him was a huge work camp containing more than two thousand human souls. Hideous and semi-savage, it rapidly grew into the largest lumbering centre on the river. Its streets were muddy tracks leading from sawmills to taverns, and drunken brawling made them dangerous after dark. Bytown endured everything. Its filth was such that even typhus developed, and in 1847 an epidemic nearly decimated the population. Cholera was common and typhoid even more so. Then, only a few years after the name of the place had been changed to "Ottawa", its fortune brightened. In 1857 Queen Victoria nominated Ottawa as the capital of United Canada.

The decision was not as absurd as it looked. If at last the two old rivals, Upper and Lower Canada, were to have a common government, a seat for it must be found in which neither province was favoured at the expense of the other. Quebec and Montreal were ruled out because the former was almost totally French and the latter was largely so; Toronto because it was English. Kingston might have served had it not been so close to the American border. At that time the fear of invasion from the United States hung constantly over Canadian heads; it was this that had caused the government to build the Rideau Canal, the purpose of which was purely military. In the event of American invaders seizing the upper St. Lawrence, the British planned to move troops up the Ottawa, then down the canal to consolidate a defence about Fort Henry at the place where the St. Lawrence channel issues from Lake Ontario. So Kingston would not do. Nor would any place else, for the simple reason that Ottawa was then the only neutral community on the one river which was shared through most of its navigable length by both the provinces.

But it was a mortifying choice, just the same. American journalists, hostile to all things British and supremely contemptuous of the Canadians for clinging to poverty under the British Crown, gave hoots of merriment when they heard the news that this new united Canada, this second nation produced by the American Revolution, had decided to place its capital in one of the most notorious work camps on the continent. The English wit Goldwin Smith described Ottawa as "a sub-arctic lumber village converted by royal mandate into a political cockpit".

In the Ottawa of that time everything seemed ugly, undignified and ridiculous, even the way things were done. Splendid new Houses of Parliament were planned, but the only suitable place for them was occupied by the abandoned wooden barracks of Colonel By. Instead of tearing the barracks down and carting off the lumber, the work gangs simply dumped them wholesale over the cliff into the river. But the work continued, the Houses of Parliament were built pretty well on schedule, and in 1860 the capital of Canada received the first of what was to become a long series of royal visits. The Queen's son, Edward, Prince of Wales, arrived to lay the cornerstone of the main building.

A primitive but extremely vivid photograph recalls not only the occasion, but the nature of Ottawa in those days. The Prince stands there, trowel in hand and with no expression on his Hanoverian countenance. About him is a semicircle of politicians in top hats and frock coats. But the scene, so far as this photograph is concerned, is stolen by the citizenry. There they are, hundreds of workmen in shirts and checked trousers, ankle deep in mud, all set to give three cheers the moment the old Bytown Brass Band has finished playing "God Save The Prince of Wales".

Now most of the human aspects of the Ottawa Valley have changed out of recognition. The lovely seigneury of the old rebel Papineau has become a famous luxury hotel. The lumbermen in the forests eat as well as eighteenth-century gentry, and Ottawa has become the most sedate city in the land. All has changed, apparently, except the old habit of taking the Ottawa River for granted, and this brings me to a story which illustrates better than anything else what the results of that habit can be.

In 1960 the Supreme Court of Canada had to consider one of the most complex and romantic cases ever to come before a Canadian bench, and the Ottawa River was the cause of it.

A few years ago the Hydro Electric Commission of Ontario decided to build a dam to enlarge the lake in the Joachims sector, the site of portages numbers 14 and 15 in the days of the voyageurs. Despite the protests of some lumbering interests, agreement was reached between the Ontario and Quebec governments and the dam was completed. The Ottawa now has a new lake, most of it artificial, some ninety miles long. As the river's current is now dead in the lake, lumbermen must tow their logs in barrel booms instead of driving them, and this greatly increases their costs. Naturally they took legal action for compensation, but at the beginning of the case neither plaintiff nor defendant seems to have been aware of the entanglements into which the ancient history of the Ottawa River would leave them before the case was settled.

For the Ottawa in this section not only belongs equally to Quebec and Ontario; many of the rights along the river depend on leases older than Confederation. Here, as is inevitable, English Common Law as practised in Ontario clashes with the old Civil Code in force in Quebec.

Nor is this all, for the practice of driving logs down rivers is much older than the discovery of Canada. Log-driving, which most Canadians assume is native, goes all the way back to Biblical times: "And Hiram sent unto Solomon, saying . . . I will do all thy desire concerning timber of cedar and concerning timber of fir. My servants shall bring them from Lebanon unto the sea: and I will convey them by floats unto the place that thou shalt appoint me."

Log-driving was never practised in England and was unknown in the continent of Europe until 1549, when it was introduced into France. A century later the Intendant Jean Talon introduced the practice into North America when he had logs driven down the St. Maurice and the St. Lawrence to Quebec. Although the Ottawa River received little settlement in the French regime, it seems certain that the French drove logs on this river in the 1740s, so that Philemon Wright was not the first man to introduce lumbering there. He certainly adopted the practice of log-driving from the French; for that matter so did all the English; it was, in modern times, a French invention.

Hence it comes about that this case between the Ontario Hydro Electric Commission and the Upper Ottawa Improvement Company is heavily involved with a cluster of French legal practices antedating not only Confederation, but even the Conquest. The Supreme Court was handed a case where some of the legal concepts lie completely outside the scope of English Common Law; where some of them, in fact, go all the way back to legal precedents which first were developed in the time of Henri IV. How valid these are I would not know. But it fascinates me to think that the history and locality of the Ottawa River have compelled their Lordships to consider them.

Of all the streams I have studied in Canada west of the Maritimes, the Ottawa on its lower reaches is the gentlest. Except in the rapids it flows calmly; birds haunt its many marshes; the water sighs through billions of reeds and past pleasant green islets. In summer along the river near Papineauville the whole scene appears, sometimes, to be resting in a trance.

But from the air you see a different prospect, and on the whole a truer one. You see the Ottawa as a strong avenue equal almost to the master stream of the present system. In broad curves it sweeps into the north-west, and from the air you see it as a boundary clear and absolute between the settled country of gentle Ontario and the Laurentian wilderness which, in all likelihood, will always remain as uncultivated as it was in the time the Algonquins hunted in it.

The Red

SASKATCHEWAN

MANITOBA

Nelson River

L. WINNIPEGOSIS

LAKE WINNIPEG

L. MANITOBA

Qu'Appelle R.

Assiniboine River

Winnipeg R.

WINNIPEG
(FT. GARRY) .SELKIRK
ST. BONIFACE

LAKE
OF THE WOODS

PEMBINA

RAIN

NORTH DAKOTA

Red River

GRAND
FORKS

UPPER RED
LOWER RED

FARGO

BRECKENRIDGE

MINNESOT

LAKE WINNIPEG

NETLEY MARSHES

ST. PA

PETERSFIELD

Red River

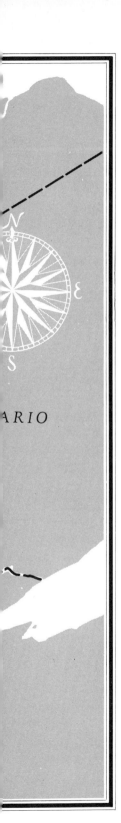

The Red

It is a tragedy of English letters that Rudyard Kipling's values were such that most of us feel we should apologize if we quote him. Actually, he had some remarkable insights. Such a phrase as "What do they know of England, who only England know?" may have been used originally as a mingled boast and sneer, but the idea behind it is universal. It can be applied to any country, province or city on earth; it can even be applied to individuals. What do we know of ourselves, if we know no other people but our own families?

Kipling's well-worn sentence has constantly come to my mind in connection with the prairies. If a person has lived solely on the prairie, I don't think he can really know it — not in the context of the general human experience — unless he has lived elsewhere for a while. That is why nearly all novels of prairie life have been written by prairie people who moved to cities in the east.

But the reverse also holds true, at least in my own case. Having grown up in a little province by the sea, its experience to some extent recorded by the literatures of maritime peoples from the Greeks to the English, I was appalled when I first found myself on the prairie. It was as alien to me as the moon's surface. I wondered how anyone could endure life in a land which seemed to me so stark. Later on I realized that what I really feared here was the idea of my own littleness. Later still I learned that the prairie's monotony contains inner beauties and harmonies as subtle as those of a Bach fugue. But it is a challenge to the soul, just the same. It is also a challenge to the eye.

For the prairie can be wonderfully beautiful, once we have learned how to look at it. That is why Frederick Philip Grove's *Along Prairie Trails* is such a haunting book, a book so much more impressive than his novels. The beauty of the prairie sky is in it, and the mystery of the prairie winter. But I myself had to be on the prairie for a while before I could see it as Grove did. My whole attitude toward alien regions altered when I heard the prairie sing. And so to the Red River.

Before I became acquainted with the Red, I shared the general belief that it is the dullest river in Canada. It is not, of course. It is the most surprising river we have in the whole land. It is unlike any other I know.

To look casually at the Red in Winnipeg nobody would ever think this. Brown and lazy, it twines through the flat city with the motion of a convolvulus and then it wanders out again into the apparent sameness of the Manitoba plain. Not even after it has received the Assiniboine does its appearance alter much, for though the Assiniboine virtually doubles its volume, the difference in the river's size passes almost unnoticed in the huge land through which it flows. In Winnipeg the Assiniboine looks like the Red's identical twin, and before the two streams join in the city's heart, strangers frequently mistake one for the other. But from the air you can see quite a difference in their characters. Seen from above, the Red looks like a brown worm wriggling directly north through the grass. The Assiniboine, seen from above, has something of a sweep to its course: it swings out of sight across the western horizon with an air of adventure.

The Red River is not really a system, though it does have its tributaries. Nor, as North American rivers go, is it long. From its southern source in Minnesota to its discharge into Lake Winnipeg its total length is only 555 miles, some fifty miles less than the length of its chief so-called tributary, the Assiniboine. The parent stream issues from Traverse Lake in Minnesota under the name of Bois de Sioux, and when this little stream unites with the Otter Tail in the small town of Breckenridge, the Red River proper begins. In the United States they call it the Red River of the North to distinguish it from the larger Red River which joins the Mississippi in Louisiana.

Once the Red finds its true course, it proceeds directly north according to the map, but does so with a steady wriggling motion worthy of the ancient Meander. Sleek and muddy, its current is so sluggish that a strong contrary wind can bring it to a halt. Its banks are ominously low, and for nearly all of its course the Red seems utterly undramatic in normal seasons. It forms some of the boundary between Minnesota and South Dakota, and all of the boundary between Minnesota and North Dakota. It wriggles through Fargo, through Grand Forks, through a number of tank towns hard to tell apart into which farmers of Yankee, Scandinavian, Teutonic and east-European origin drive from the prairie to attend church or the little movie house, to buy necessities and discuss prices of wheat, to grumble about the weather and listen to juke-boxes in restaurants operated by Greeks, Chinese or anyone else who does not want to be a farmer. These main-street towns below the border have changed hardly at all since Sinclair Lewis wrote about Gopher Prairie. But they do have the Red River, which Gopher Prairie did not. The Red wriggles on, picking up a number of small prairie streams, most of them dried out in summer, all of them in rainy springs cataracting into the main channel in sluices of liquid mud. Just below the little town of Pembina, which claims to be "historical" and actually is (though the passing traveller would never guess so from its appearance), the Red crawls across the international border into Canada. Barely a quarter of its length is in Manitoba, but these final miles are by far the most interesting along the river's course.

I find myself able to describe the Red in general terms only in a series of paradoxes.

The first is the contrast between its colour and that of the prairie through which it flows: the prairie here is not red at all, but charcoal black. The reason for the Red's colour is the depth of its trench. It is a shallow trench compared to the Saskatchewan's — a most important point in the river's history — but deep enough to lie well below the black topsoil in which the Manitoba wheat grows. It is carved right into a subsoil clay which bakes hard in drought and in rain turns into a thick gumbo soup slippery enough to ski on.

The second paradox is more difficult to make clear, for to me it was the most surprising of all: the Red River, more than any other stream I have seen outside of England, reminds me of the Thames. As this statement would have sounded incredible if anyone had made it to me a dozen years ago, I should explain what I mean.

Manitoba is as unlike southern England as any country you

could find outside high mountain ranges. Southern England is Constable country, and who could imagine Constable painting a Manitoba sectional farm? The southern English landscape is the subtlest, probably, in the world, and its valleys have enchanted the poets for centuries. But the Red River Valley is not a valley at all as people usually understand the meaning of that word. It is a colossal plain table-flat. Ocean-like in size, but flatter than any ocean because it has no waves, it is black in spring, golden in August, white in winter. Its sole companion is a vast sky constantly changing above it, constantly moving above it.

Yet in this apparently stark setting the Red River again and again creates little aquatic scenes of pure loveliness. Splendid trees follow its banks sloping down with some undergrowth from the prairie table to the water's edge. As you drive along the plain and see these trees, if you did not know what caused them, you would never guess a river was there. You come to the river suddenly; you walk or drive along the flatness, and abruptly you are at its trench. And more than once, standing on the prairie table to look down at a reach of the Red, I thought of the great reach the Thames makes at Goring. Once where an apron of soft green grass stretched out into the water, I even remembered Runnymede.

Then there is the delta. It contains more than a hundred square miles of brown marsh grass and water, with a few willows interspersed. Its expanse is as flat as the rest of Manitoba and it is virtually uninhabited. As you near the forks where the three main channels of the river wind through the sedge into Lake Winnipeg, this empty region alive with swirling birds can seem as awe-inspiring as the lonely delta of the Slave. It can be incredibly beautiful, too. In late autumn and early winter the northern lights have a habit of rising above it, and their weird light, filtering through the man-high marsh grass, translates this whole region out of the world, translates it into patterns of unearthly lumination shifting through a landscape out of which all life has vanished save for the muskrats, otters, beavers and fish. For when the brightest auroras shine, the birds of the delta have flown south.

Yet in this same delta, miles from any settlement, on a fine spring afternoon I found myself in a channel so small, still, intimate and fragrant that I thought of the most civilized stream I know, the tiny Cherwell curving through may blossoms and bird songs under the wall of Magdalen, under Magdalen Bridge, and then through Christ Church meadows to the Thames. I could almost dream I was back there. Then there was a sharp slap on the water and the lad who was steering my boat rose and pointed. We had come to a beaver dam and the beaver had gone under water to hide.

The Red has other contrasts of a general nature, and not all of them are charming. This same river I have called both gentle and awe-inspiring can also, in its higher reaches, look as squalid as a dried-out irrigation ditch in certain seasons and vicissitudes of climate. During the great drought of 1934 there was a period of six months when the Red above Winnipeg virtually disappeared. In all that time not even a bucketful of water went through Fargo, though Fargo is about 150 miles from its source. When winds blew they set clouds of dust smoking along the river's trench, which seemed the most blighted part of the whole parched land.

Sixteen years later the Red ceased to be a river once more, but this time it turned itself into a lake.

Now, to combine all these contrasts into the single one which is the principal cause of the others — the Red behaves in this contradictory way because, geologically speaking, it is not a river at all. It is a surviving remnant of what once was the largest freshwater lake in existence, at least in recent geological history.

Lake Agassiz — so the geologists call it after the Swiss scientist who studied the movements of icecaps — was the product of the last of the glaciers which shaped the present form of the central Canadian plain, together with much of Minnesota, all of North Dakota and most of South Dakota. It is with the origins of Lake Agassiz that everyone must begin who wishes to understand the nature of the central prairie, of the prairie lakes and of the Red River itself. The time to begin is a million years ago (a recent date in geological history) because it was then that the first Ice Age began. Since that time there have been four major advances and retreats of the polar ice cap in America, and the effects of them all are plainly visible in Manitoba today.

The prairie was not always as it is now. Once it was a normal, rolling land very like the terrain between Ottawa and Lake Ontario, with hills and depressions and little streams. But as quadrillions of tons of ice formed on it, the weight of the ice slowly crushed the land, and when the ice moved, it shaved off every hill and depression until the prairie as we know it was formed. In its progress south, the ice finally pressed against the height of land which extends just south of Traverse Lake in Minnesota, and there it stopped. This small elevation, today crossed almost unnoticed by thousands of tourists in their cars, is one of the most important land-heights in North America, for it is the north-south continental divide. It is the reason why the Missouri curves to the southeast to join the Mississippi, and why the Red and all the Canadian rivers flow toward the north.

But — and this is another curious contradiction in the Red's history — there was a time when the Red *did* flow south. While the glacier still existed in the north, south was the only way some of the water of Lake Agassiz could go, so there was a dribble over the continental shelf which eventually found its way into the Mississippi.

Now picture the scene in central Canada as it was during the many thousand years when the climate was growing warmer and the ice was melting. As the glacier withdrew and the southern ice turned into water, this water was captured in a basin bounded in the south by the height of land which now is the north-south divide, and in the north by the still existing wall of glacial ice. This huge catch-pit was Lake Agassiz, and for several aeons the Red — as has been explained — drained some of it off in a southerly direction.

In the period of its greatest extent, Lake Agassiz was more than seven hundred miles long and two hundred and fifty miles wide. Its total area exceeded that of the combined five Great Lakes today. It covered northern Minnesota, the north-eastern sections of South Dakota, and pretty well all of Manitoba. Until the ice retreated far enough into the north to enable the water to be carried off by Hudson Bay — the proximity of the bay explains why the glacier finally went off so quickly — Lake Agassiz drained into Lake Superior and for a time was a part of the St. Lawrence system, some of its waters reaching the Atlantic past Quebec.

As the glacier continued to retreat, mastodons and primitive men lived along the shores of Lake Agassiz, and the remains of millions of dead organisms sank to the bottom to enrich what later became the dry land the settlers put to the plough. Not until ten to fifteen thousand years ago — only yesterday in the time-span of a geologist — did the main body of Lake Agassiz finally disappear. Behind it remain sizable bodies of water called Lakes Winnipeg, Winnipegosis, Manitoba, the Upper and Lower Red Lakes, Lake of the Woods, Rainy Lake and that maze of mosquito-breeding ponds, sloughs and midget-sized lakes in the western Shield. Also there remained two important rivers, the Nelson and the Red. Today the Red, joined by lazy tributaries, worms through the central bed of old Lake Agassiz.

That is why, when certain weather conditions conspire, the Red River reverts atavistically to the behaviour of the lake which fathered it. In simpler language, when the Red floods there is hardly anything the people can do to stop it under present conditions. You can fight an ordinary river by means of dykes and levees, but nobody can stem the overflow of a river which turns itself into a lake on a continental plain where the highest elevation seldom exceeds twelve feet.

In the early spring of 1852, David Anderson, Bishop of Rupert's Land, was able to reflect with some reason that religion, civilization and tradition were taking root in the enormous frontier diocese under his care. In his school near old Fort Garry one pupil had just completed the reading of Aristotle's *Ethics* in the original Greek. Several others had worked their way through Herodotus into Thucydides, four lads were studying the Gospels in Italian, most of the school knew them in French, and the whole school had recited a psalm in Hebrew and the Lord's Prayer in eight different languages "including the two leading dialects of our country". For a thousand miles around this little human island the wilderness and the empty plain extended, but within the colony itself the farms were prosperous, families were at least earning a livelihood, and the desperate hardships of the early days along the Red River were becoming memories.

But into this scene of peace, like a tocsin, came tidings the settlers dreaded, for they knew from experience what was coming to them. At Pembina, a hundred-odd miles to the south, the Red River was beginning to flood. Communications were slow and inadequate, and at first nobody knew for certain how serious the situation was. But they did know the habits of the river. The Red moves slowly, heavily, but with a fatal sureness. By May 2 the situation at Fort Garry was alarming and people began leaving their homes. The first bridges went as the river swelled, and a controlled anguish of panic was framed, as it were, in a scene of perfect peace. On May 8, Bishop Anderson noted that "the aurora borealis was brilliant at night, like a semi-circular arch of tailed comets". The next day he "awoke to the sweet singing of birds, and soon heard the news that the waters were stationary at Pembina".

But they were not stationary, as the Bishop soon discovered.

"There has been today a peculiar noise, like the sound of many waters, such as one may imagine the distant sound of Niagara: it was the pouring of water over the plains." So sudden, so immense, was this flood that some of the settlers could not believe that a stream as innocent-looking as the Red could contain all that water. "They thought the Missouri was coming down on them," the Bishop noted in his diary.

But May 10 was another beautiful morning of singing birds, though the water was now flooding into the granaries and stores, and the people were working frantically to save the food on which they depended for their lives that summer. The Red River colony, even as late as 1852, was the most isolated civilized settlement in America; if catastrophe came to it, there was nobody but themselves to whom the people could look for help. The day passed into a bright Manitoba evening, but now the churchyard, "the seedplot of God", was entirely covered, and everywhere houses were awash or floating away. Three days later the Bishop noted that a tempest arose in the night, and that the resurrected Lake Agassiz roared like the sea. On Sunday a few days after the storm, Bishop Anderson's congregation rowed or paddled to a spot of dry land on the edge of the waters and there he preached a sermon on the destruction of Sodom and Gomorrah. At evensong on that same day he preached on Noah's dove, and the choir, standing in the open, "sang most beautifully Spofforth's *Te Deum*".

But the waters, oblivious of the prayers of the people and the sermons of the Bishop, deepened, gained and spread. On May 17 a boat was rowed through the churchyard gate and across the plain until it blundered into the main channel of the river, now foaming with a velocity of ten knots, and the boat was nearly lost in it. Wreckage floating everywhere reminded the Bishop to quote from the storm scene in the first book of Vergil's *Aeneid: Arma virumque tabulaeque et Troia gaza per undas* — "the arms of men, pictures and Trojan treasures in the waves". Now men, women and children were drowning, cattle were floating feet up, stoves and ploughs lashed to rafts had been carried away and lost forever, some of them swept by the current down through the delta into Lake Winnipeg itself. But when dry land was reached, "violets and buttercups, raspberry and strawberry blossoms were grateful to the eye", and beyond the water's brink Bishop Anderson saw men who had saved both ploughs and oxen working to the point of exhaustion to turn the sod before it would be too late to plant a crop. Mosquitoes, thriving in the dampness, formed clouds as thick as midges.

Four days later the flood reached its height and became stationary, and the Bishop, hoisting a sail in his "birch-rind canoe", went for a long voyage across the prairie in beautiful weather. The farmland was now transformed into a lake several hundred miles long and about twelve miles wide, with maples in full leaf protruding from it and birds singing in the branches, the gables of houses projecting from the water and families floating about in boats and on rafts. At 3:00 a.m. the next day "the sunrise was like a sunrise at sea", with the addition of the bird songs and the fresh green of the trees. Another Sabbath came. The day before it the Bishop had seen a flag hoisted to signify that the flood was abating, so his text was from Isaiah: "When the enemy shall come in like a flood, the spirit of the Lord shall lift up a standard against him." A few days after this, as the Bishop noted in still another Latin quotation, land began to appear above the waters. Quickly the waters drained off leaving a sea of slime which the sun soon baked to a scum, and into this miserable land the tired people returned.

Three weeks after the height of the flood, the first boats of the Long Portage brigade passed Fort Garry on their way west via the Saskatchewan to meet the brigades descending from the Mackenzie fifteen hundred miles away. With them they brought American newspapers from the south which told of a recent flood in Yorkshire in which nearly a hundred lives were lost. The Bishop reflected thankfully that the Lord had dealt with them graciously here, that "now the melody of former times may be renewed", and that in the future, when he took his seat in the hall where the daily worship was held, there would be "behind me the same engraving as before, that from the original of Andrea Sacchi, of Noah rearing his altar of thanksgiving, when saved from the waters of the flood."

This mid-nineteenth century description of a Red River flood can serve well for a record of nearly all of them. The flood described by Bishop Anderson was worse than the one in 1950, the last severe flood on record at the time of writing, but the behaviour of the Red River in all of its floods has been pretty much the same, and will likely be similar in the future. From 1776 to 1950 included, the Red has flooded seriously a dozen times, made a nuisance of itself often and not once has it successfully been com-

bated. On each separate occasion the causes of a flood have been the same.

The first is the sluggish pace of the current: the drop in the Red from Fargo to Lake Winnipeg is so slight that the river's trench cannot carry off more than a normal quantity of water in a given time. The second cause is a series of heavy autumn rains followed by a quick frost which freezes the moisture into the prairie, preserving it for future action in the spring. Quick frosts of this sort are very frequent here; sometimes they occur in the first week of October and remain. The next cause is heavy winter snow. If these two latter acts of God are followed by a late spring, a sudden prolonged thaw and heavy spring rains, the Red (in the words of Ralph Allen when he described in *Maclean's* the flood of 1950) "can't possibly miss". It turns itself into a miniature Lake Agassiz, and not all the technology of modern man has so far been able to avert the usual consequences.

In the flood of 1950, some 100,000 Canadians and 20,000 Americans were driven from their homes, fifteen thousand farm buildings and business blocks were inundated, and the loss of life might have been serious had not the Canadian Army taken over. On that occasion, as Winnipeg people vividly recall, the Army was prepared to declare martial law and remove 320,000 civilians according to the plan which would have been used in southern England in 1940 if the Nazis had crossed the Channel.

This plan may have to be put into effect next year or five years hence, for Winnipeg is as defenceless against the Red River as it has always been. The stream looks so innocent; yet – because it is a survival of a lake – it can become deadly. As early as 1880, when Sir Sandford Fleming was in charge of the survey for the Canadian Pacific Railway, he recommended that the railway crossing of the Red should be located twenty miles below Winnipeg where the banks are higher and the flooding less serious. Winnipeg at that time was a small community and might easily have been moved, but people learn little from past experience and the citizens decided to remain where they were.

When I was in Winnipeg in 1960 making a special study of the Red, it so happened that a convention of engineers was held in the hotel at the same time. One of my uncles, an engineer who has done a good deal of work in connection with the Saskatchewan, showed me the proceedings of the conference. The engineers recommended the construction of a floodway to divert the overflow around greater Winnipeg, and perhaps in the near future their plans will be adopted. On the maps they looked practical enough, but the cost would be prodigious. So, for that matter, would be the cost of a first-class flood. The 1950 affair was far from the worst on the record – on that occasion the Assiniboine held off until the Red had done its worst – but it cost $110 million in losses alone.

People in the east think of the three prairie provinces as similar and lump them together under the general term "the West". Yet their histories are quite different. The Red River Valley, in antiquity of settlement, is much older than Saskatchewan and Alberta. Though all three provinces have a common background of fur trading, though the Vérendrye family explored them all (the elder LaVérendrye established Fort Rouge at the forks of the Red and Assiniboine in 1738) it is a fact of some significance that the homesteaders of the two westernmost provinces had the railways behind them at least most of the way, and that the nineteenth century was two-thirds over before serious farming began in Saskatchewan. But the Red River Valley settlement not only dates back to an earlier period in the story of western America; it emerged from an earlier stage in the social and moral evolution of the Europe from which the settlers came.

This is not the place to tell the story of the Selkirk Settlement, the full implications of which were greater than have been expressed in any local history of the Settlement I have so far read. The story of the Settlement began across the ocean. Originally, the conditions which made the Settlement seem reasonable to Lord Selkirk arose out of conditions shameful to the ruling classes of the British Isles, whether English, Scottish or Irish.

Well before the end of the eighteenth century, the Highland Scotch were virtually finished as a force within their own land. Isolated for centuries in mountains which could never support a large population, living in warring clans ruled by patriarchal chiefs intensely jealous and for the most part devoid of intelligence, the Highlanders had believed they were braver than anyone else, and in the physical sense they possibly were braver than most. But it was not their valour which had kept their antiquated system intact for so long; it was the poverty of their country. Had it been worth enough, English and Lowland cannon would have taken it from them. A people whose concept of valour was the same as that of Achilles could never have held out against the military tactics even of a seventeenth-century English army. Montrose, after all, was not a Highlander. Though it is true that only Highland or Montenegrin troops could have endured as his did, their endurance would have availed nothing if Montrose's leadership had been of the usual Highland kind. Nothing was more typical of the old Highland mentality than the behaviour of their most powerful clan at the battle of Culloden in 1745. The Macdonalds, placed by blunder or jealousy on the left wing, refused to fight because the post of honour on the right had been given to another clan. Homer would have understood such people; indeed, he described them better than any Scottish writer has ever done, for he was not a sentimentalist.

No sane Scotsman could blame the English for treating the Highlanders as they did after the 1745 rebellion. Their blind loyalty to their chiefs, who in turn were blindly loyal to a worthless Pretender, had given the English no choice save to uproot and destroy the ancient clan system.

But these Highlanders were magnificent human material, and what was done to them when they were helpless was as disgraceful as what was done to the poor Irish by rack-renting landlords and stupid aristocratic brutes like Lord Lucan. They were enclosed so that landlords might turn the glens into sheep runs, and many of the landlords who committed this crime were not English, but Scotch. If the crimes committed against them were not denounced as were the crimes committed against the Irish, it was because the Highlanders took so long to be weaned from the family concept of society in which they were reared. Most of them covered up the selfish callousness of the chiefs who were supposed to be their fathers. They were too ashamed of them to complain in public after they were deported overseas to Canada or Australia, or left to starve. Seldom did a Highlander place the blame where it belonged, as did the unknown Canadian voyageur who wrote, somewhere on the western rivers, that he and his kind were exiles from their native land "that a degenerate lord might boast his sheep". Yet even this poet, in the one verse of his song which everyone knows, uttered the permanent Highland home-sickness which stopped their lips from the final denunciation:

> *From the lone shieling of the misty island*
> *Mountains divide us, and the waste of seas —*
> *But still the blood is strong, the heart is Highland,*
> *And we in dreams behold the Hebrides.*

There was something Judaic in the Scotch of the north, just as there was something Judaic in their fate, and in their ultimate triumph when finally they learned to master the techniques and the culture of their conquerors. What Scotland lost, Canada was to gain: and Australia, New Zealand and the United States also, but in proportion more was gained by Canada.

For these reasons it is difficult for anyone of Scotch descent to sneer at Lord Selkirk, despite what his recklessness, and at times his arrogance, did to many people. Lord Selkirk was one of the very few chiefs of his time who felt a genuine compassion for his people, and made it his life's work to help them. While everyone recognized that the old clan way of life had become economically impossible, and that ultimately most of the Highlanders would have to leave the glens, Selkirk at least tried to find a home for them. We can imagine him looking at the maps which were coming from the New World, perhaps even talking with Highlanders who had been west with the canoes, or with Orkneymen of the Hudson's Bay Company. We can imagine the great idea forming in his mind: across the sea, on the empty Canadian plain, was all the land his land-hungry people could desire, so why not send them there? But like many honest idealists, Selkirk was not informed of the realities his people would encounter on that empty plain.

More than once the Napoleonic Wars exercised an influence on Canadian history, but never more ironically than they did now. The Emperor's Berlin Decrees had all but ruined the fur market. When it was impossible to ship furs into the continent, the stock of the Hudson's Bay Company dropped from £250 a share to £60. Lord Selkirk saw his opportunity. Though he had no interest in the fur trade, he had a most lively interest in the country the Gentlemen Adventurers claimed to own. Taking advantage of the low price of shares, he bought control of the Hudson's Bay Company. Then he chartered a few small ships, filled them with homeless Celts, placed the party under the leadership of a stubborn man called Miles Macdonnell, and sent them with his blessing across the western ocean bound through Hudson Strait to York Factory at the foot of Hudson Bay.

In 1811 the first band of settlers reached York Factory, and there they wintered. The next summer they paddled seven hundred and fifty miles south up the Nelson River, then up Lake Winnipeg and the Red to its confluence with the Assiniboine. Though they did not know it, during those same weeks Napoleon was leading his *grande armée* across a land equally flat, and potentially almost as cold, from Smolensk to Moscow. Although the settlers were very few, and Napoleon's army more than half a million men, their experiences the following winter were not dissimilar.

No body of settlers in Canada ever endured more prolonged or terrifying suffering than did the Selkirk people. Idealists are seldom good planners, and Lord Selkirk was no exception to this general rule. His people arrived without ploughs, and pathetically they tried to scratch the surface of that gigantic plain with hoes and spades. Their sole line of communication ran back seven hundred and fifty miles to a tiny fort visited once a year by ships making a dangerous passage from home. Soon they were starving. Almost as bad as that, soon they were engaged in a civil war with the men of the North West Company, who themselves were engaged in a desperate struggle for survival against the Bay.

Settlement, as the Nor'westers always knew, is fatal to the fur trade, and here was a settlement encamped across their lines of communication. The Nor'westers attacked the homes of the settlers and burned some of them to the ground. The Indians, perhaps urged on by the fur-traders, attacked and killed some of them. In the Red River delta I have been shown hollows in the ground where some of the Selkirk people concealed their children, placing sods or marsh grass over them, when the Indians attacked. But somehow the core of the settlement survived.

For nine awful years, while Lord Selkirk, driven almost mad by a mixture of compassion, anger and guilt, fought with the leaders of the North West Company, the wretched farmers on the Red River struggled to keep alive. They roamed up and down the river in search of buffalo. A decade after their arrival, small numbers of French Canadians appeared, made their little settlement at St. Boniface opposite Fort Garry, and shared the existence of their Scottish brothers. In 1826 the Red River itself rose against them, and in the worst flood recorded in its history, it washed away nearly all the meagre homes they had. For shelter, the survivors could only dig cellars in the plain, roof them with sods, and live through the winters under ground.

They persevered because this was all they could do. To return home was impossible. Summer was "a time of peace with hunger", winter a six months' white hell. In 1837 a plague of grasshoppers ate their crop and left them without seed for the next year. The winter following, two heroes walked a thousand miles to a point on the Mississippi where they believed that seed could be bought. They returned with two hundred bushels of wheat seed, a hundred of oats and thirty of peas, and for the whole lot Lord Selkirk paid out of his own purse $600. Years later one of their descendants wrote: "Almost one might say that the Lord blessed that seed, for it saved the settlement."

The Settlement which then grew and burgeoned was unique in America. Though the wilderness extended for a thousand miles in every direction around it, the moment the people "could eat their bread without weight and their potatoes without measure", schools and churches rose among them, books were imported from England, and some of their teachers were men trained in Edinburgh, Oxford and Cambridge. In 1855, only three years after the flood described by Bishop David Anderson, an American journalist visited the Red River and on his return he wrote the following:

"There is a spot on this continent which travellers do not visit. Deserts, almost trackless, divide it from the habitations of men. To reach it, or once there to escape it, is an exploit of which one may almost boast. It is not even marked on the maps nor mentioned in the gazetteers."

Yet at the forks of the Red and the Assiniboine, this American visitor wrote that he had found dancing and good dining, several excellent wine cellars, one library, copies of *The Illustrated London News*, the latest novels of Dickens and Thackeray. "Intellectual conversation," he wrote, "might be had there as well as in Washington."

All these books, wines and cultural influences had come to the Red River *from the north!*

The Settlement remained isolated until several years after Confederation, its lines of communication now running south toward the head of steel in St. Paul. But one April day in 1871, there came floating down to Fort Garry a wooden scow loaded with eight men. They were "Canadians from Ontario"; they had bought the scow in the United States and come down the Red River aboard it intending to homestead on the plains. Though neither they nor the original settlers knew this at the time, those eight men were the advance guard of the homesteading avalanche which was to doom the fur trade, cause the two Riel Rebellions, accelerate the building of the Canadian Pacific Railway, and, by the century's end, turn the bed of Lake Agassiz into one of the richest wheat-producing regions on earth.

Today the Red River Valley is no longer "the West"; it is the geographical heart of Canada. It may also be the ethnic and social heart as well.

Here, facing one another across the river, are the two communities of Winnipeg and St. Boniface, one palpably Scotch-English-Canadian, the other palpably French-Canadian. But around these two original cores, indeed threaded through them, are the lines of a mosaic of peoples whose origins stem from all the nations of the Old World. In the little town of Selkirk just below the lower and larger Fort Garry, you can see this mosaic plain. The most prominent building is an onion-domed Ukrainian church. But within a stone's throw of it is a street called Britannia Avenue, the Anglican house of worship is called Christ Church, and there is even a street called after Toronto. In lower Fort Garry itself the style of stone cutting is pure Old Country, and the Fort is as authentically British colonial as York Redoubt at the mouth of Halifax Harbour, which was built at the turn of the eighteenth century into the nineteenth, and named after

> *The good old Duke of York,*
> *He had ten thousand men;*
> *He marched them up to the top of the hill*
> *And he marched them down again.*

This continuance of tradition in the Red River Valley, it seems to me, has been and still is of priceless value. It has been one of the factors which saved Canada from becoming an amorphous melting pot with all sense lost of our ancestors' cultures in the Old World. Winnipeg has never seemed really provincial to me. For years, when John Dafoe was its editor, the Winnipeg *Free Press* was one of the most admired newspapers in the Commonwealth, and it spoke with an authority heard even in London. It seems to me a fact that the French-speaking people of Manitoba are less provincial in their attitude than are those of the parent province of Quebec. Did not St. Boniface give to French Canada its finest prose writer in the person of Gabrielle Roy, who discovered Balzac as a little girl and became the first writer not a citizen of France to receive the *prix femina*?

Yet the Red River, though its settlements are now fairly old by western standards and barely four hours by air from Montreal, can still appear in one region so pristine that when you are there you can feel yourself the only man alive in the world.

Last spring I drove in a rented car to the delta, turned off at Petersfield into a little track leading inward, and came to its end in the Netley Marshes. It was the beginning of one of the finest days of my life, for there, at the end of the road, I found a camp with motor boats owned by a Canadian of Polish ancestry called Ed Chesley. When I told him I wanted to see the delta, there appeared in his face that look of friendship one sometimes sees in a man when a stranger reveals interest in the thing he loves. Quietly he asked his son Larry to prepare a boat, and while the fuel was being poured into the tank, we talked. It happened to be a few days after the U-2 affair; so for a time, we had more to talk about than the geography of the delta. But here the antics of the politicians soon dwindled into insignificance. Under that vast sky, in this huge region of marsh grass and wildfowl, what were the politicians in Paris that anyone should be mindful of them?

"There is so much to know here," Mr. Chesley said. "We spend our winters in Florida now, and I think I know every branch of the Everglades. But it is wilder here, and there is more here. There is much, much more."

He told me of the Brokenhead Indian reservation just to the east of the delta, and a little about the flocks of birds. It was also he who showed me the depressions in the ground where the Selkirk settlers had hidden their children. Then his son called out that the boat was ready, I joined him, and Larry led me into the best duck-breeding area in North America.

The Red River delta, flat as the plain to the south of it, flat as the lake to the north of it, is an astonishingly large delta for a river relatively small. But the Red, one must remember, carries an abnormally large weight of silt in its waters. In that labyrinth of channels twisting through reeds and swamps a greenhorn would lose himself in fifteen minutes. But young Larry Chesley knew the delta as a man knows his own property. He took me into channel after channel while ducks of every species skittered away over the surface, or broke cover and took to the air. Marsh hawks, brilliant of colour and the size of eagles, beat slowly back and forth over that sea of reeds in which mice, rats, muskrats, otters, beavers and fish lurk. Herons stood on one leg in shallow places; bush after bush was spangled with scarlet from the wings of roosting red-winged blackbirds; huge white pelicans, some of them weighing up to fifty pounds, floated on the water or rose with slow, heavy flappings of wings. We found the course of the Red River, sailed down it for a time, then turned off into one of its many little side channels – the one which reminded me of the Cherwell – went through the beaver dam I mentioned before and came out to another expanse where a game-warden's wooden tower stood in the marsh and in the flatness seemed as high as a skyscraper. We climbed it. Then in this new solitude the whole air was full of birdsongs for miles about, it vibrated with them, and as we returned to the boat a flight of mallard broke cover and flew away.

"In the fall," Larry said, "duck hunters come here from every place, and we take them out into the marshes. They jump-shoot from boats, or they shoot from blinds, or they use decoys." A little later he added: "Father and I go south after the birds leave here. Or did he tell you that? Last year in Mexico when I went shooting, some of the ducks I bagged may have been ducks I'd missed here a month earlier."

We reached the final forks of the Red where it divides into three channels, passed down the eastern branch and entered Lake Winnipeg. We coasted along toward the mouth of the central channel which is almost invisible when you are out in the lake. The flat lake spread north over the horizon, the delta south into the prairie. The afternoon enclosed us along with hundreds of thousands of large fowl and the myriads of blackbirds and larks calling and shrilling in the higher light. Larry Chesley stopped the motor, and with the sinking sun streaming over the delta into our eyes, we floated absolutely alone on that sea-like remnant of old Lake Agassiz.

The Saskatchewan

The Saskatchewan

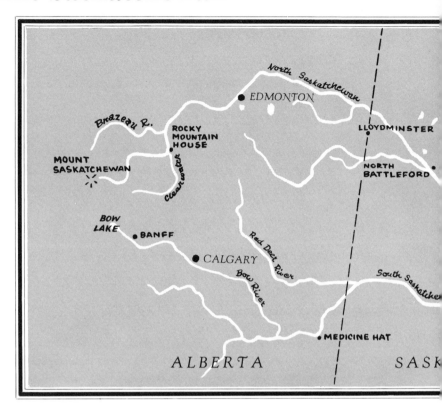

Of all the major rivers of this continent, the Saskatchewan seems to me the loneliest looking. By this I mean the concept of it, the image of it considered as a whole, for like any body of moving water the river in section after section can be sprightly and full of grace. In many places where I have sat beside it, the Saskatchewan made me think of a smooth body pulsing with life, a depth in it, a quiet tirelessness, and Mrs. Campbell has written well of the beauty of the foam which washes down along its surface like white lace.

Yet surely the Saskatchewan, when we think of it as a whole, has within its image the great solitude of the prairie it crosses. Endlessly winding, seldom dramatic between the Rockies and the final spasm at Grand Rapids, the twin branches flow through the central plain in a huge, wavering Y.

Often the Saskatchewan passes through bush and parkland, and these were the regions most prized by the fur-traders. But more often it winds through naked plains, and the feeling of lone-

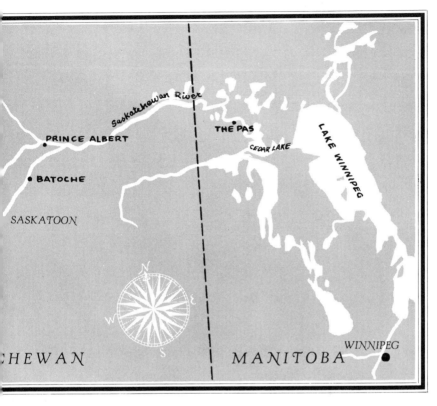

PRINCE ALBERT

BATOCHE

SASKATOON

Saskatchewan River

THE PAS

CEDAR LAKE

LAKE WINNIPEG

HEWAN

MANITOBA

WINNIPEG

liness is in proportion to the bareness of the land. The river is always below the surface of the prairie and it seldom floods, for its trenches are extremely deep. For hundreds of miles the trenches of the two branches channel the waters easterly: hundreds of miles of tan, monotonous water with weeds and wildflowers rife along the escarpments when sand-bars protrude from the channels in late summer; hundreds of miles of greenish-white ice against the flat white of the plain.in the six-month winter which seems so interminable that the people in the river towns hold sweepstakes on the hour and minute of the spring break-up. When finally the break-up comes it is the most awaited moment in the seasonal life of the Saskatchewan. The ice cracks, the floes pile up a dozen feet high and occasionally bizarre things can happen. Not long ago in Saskatoon a bewildered deer was carried through the heart of the town on an ice pan while thousands of people watched. Then, after a pause, comes the time of high water when the twin branches race with foam as they carry eastward the run-off from billions of tons of Rocky Mountain snow.

The lonely feeling given by the Saskatchewan is different from what is felt on the Mackenzie because here there are so many people. It is the nature of the prairie landscape that a human being, a house, a grain elevator, a moving train, even a village etched against the sky serve only to enhance the sense of space. Standing on the banks of the Saskatchewan, seeing it come out of one horizon on its way into another, many a newcomer must have felt he could go no further into this enormousness without losing all sense of who he was. The western Missouri used to give a similar sensation to many an American homesteader. But though the Missouri is a greater river than the Saskatchewan, it lies farther south; it does not have that final northern quality of making you feel you are on the edge of nothing human. Stepping off a train onto the wooden platform of one of those stark little Saskatchewan river towns, many a settler must have walked down to the river and watched the water coming out of the prairie into the town – so tiny and alone in that vast space – and then watched it going out again into the prairie, and wondered if he would ever be equal to his life in such a land. Some prairie people are indignant when easterners use the word "stark" to describe their towns. They shouldn't be. The very fact that towns like Prince Albert exist and thrive in a place where recently there was nothing but grass is a triumph. Can towns become cities in two lifetimes?

For along most of the Saskatchewan, whether on the North Branch or the South, the world has been reduced to what W. O. Mitchell called the least common denominator of nature, land and sky. There is also the effect of the weather. It shifts constantly and with it the moods of sky and land, and the river reflects all these moods with total fidelity. Few sights in Canada are more peaceful than the mirroring of the pastel sky-hues on the Saskatchewan on a fine summer day; none more chilling than an eddy of snow in January when the thermometer stands at forty or fifty below and the ice is too hard for a curling stone. The winds here are visible: in summer you see them as a throbbing radiance along a sea of grass, in winter as a drifting lace of ice crystals along a sea of snow.

My doctor-father used to say that nature is usually just, that what she takes with one hand she gives with the other. The Saskatchewan country can be so bleakly stern it shrivels the soul; it can also intoxicate with a deluge of prolific loveliness that makes an English June seem insipid by comparison. In the spring the voice of the turtle is not heard much in this land, but the voices and movements of a myriad of other birds, many of them water-fowl, make hundreds of miles of clear atmosphere quiver with sound and flash with colour and the very sky thrill with the larks. The sloughs teem, the land deprived by the long winter goes mad with the lust of re-creating the life the frost has killed. Moses would have understood this land. Had civilized men lived along the Saskatchewan three milleniums ago, the prairie country would have burgeoned with psalmists and prophets.

The Saskatchewan is not a simple stream but a system of waters having a combined length greater than that of the St. Lawrence or Danube and draining a basin composed of much of Alberta and Saskatchewan provinces, a little of Wyoming and some of Mani-toba. Its strategic course as the principal prairie water route has made the Saskatchewan the second most indispensable of all Canadian rivers. The voyageurs followed one branch north-west across the plain toward Portage LaTraite and the Methye, while the other branch carried them south-west into Wyoming and into the Rockies by Bow Pass.

Though most of the Saskatchewan flows through the plains, its waters rise in one of the most spectacular regions of North Amer-ica. The North Branch, fathered by the Columbia Icefield, comes out of the glacier on Mount Saskatchewan, and when you stand on the little bridge over the North Fork and look at that lithe, frigid stream, not glacial-green but milky from limestone, so narrow in August that a broad-jumper could clear it, you can have a strange sensation when you think how far this water has to go.

The analogy between rivers and lives has been overworked, but only because it is unavoidable. The beginnings of both move us more than we care to admit because they show that all things are subject to accident. A chance in the human genes, a drunken driver, a virus so small it is invisible through a microscope, and a human life is stunted or killed. A tilt in the landscape, the prox-imity of a larger stream, and what might have been a famous river is only a tributary brook.

But this milky, cold brook we see bubbling down from Mount Saskatchewan survives to claim mastery over hundreds of brooks and even a few sizable rivers. In the mountains it does not have the firm, confidence of the young Athabaska, which finds the broad Jasper Valley soon in its career. In the mountains the North Branch is a nervous river. Its grey-green waters flicker down between Mounts Amery and Coleman, its wide gravel washes are littered with the bleaching bones of dead trees carried off in spring floods, and it finds or carves a narrow course through the ranges. It flows down to Rocky Mountain House where it takes in the Brazeau and Clearwater, then it swells into the plain and flows on toward Edmonton, having gathered in several other mountain streams as it goes.

When the North Saskatchewan twists under the escarpments of Alberta's largest city, it is a master stream flecked with foam and haunted with wildfowl, it is about a hundred and forty feet wide at the bridges and the trench in places is deeper than a hundred feet. Its surface looks like tan silk, its current is visible with the life of the mountains still within it, its sound is a lisping whisper. But that this is already a river of the plains is proved by the amount of silt it carries. Floundering through ragweed and mud the colour and texture of axle-grease, I made the primitive test of holding a silver quarter under the river's surface. As it disappeared at a depth of three inches, I presumed that even here the river carries more sediment than the Red. And yet it does not look so sleek and muddy, and its flow, of course, is much more powerful.

From Edmonton the North Branch winds out into the plain through horizon after horizon with here and there a tiny village stark on its banks, and here and there a clump of cottonwood or birch. After crossing the provincial border above Lloydminster – when the first homesteaders arrived in the North Bend they found the prairie grass so rich and tangled they could scarcely walk in it – the river journeys some ten horizons farther into North Battleford. Here it takes in the Battle, bends south and then north to Prince Albert, above it the limitless sky, about and beyond it the empty land.

A little past Prince Albert, at the Forks, the North Branch finally meets its great partner from the south. Then the united Saskatchewan flows through the wilderness into Manitoba, past The Pas into Cedar Lake. Here through the ages it has deposited so much silt that Alexander Mackenzie, when he saw the region two centuries ago, predicted that in time all this watery expanse would turn into forest.

After Cedar Lake the Saskatchewan's journey is nearly done. With a swift rush of rapids, the waters swirl into the north-western bulge of Lake Winnipeg at a point some three hundred and forty miles east of the forks. Eventually some Saskatchewan water leaks out into the Nelson and reaches the brine of Hudson Bay, but it is wrong to claim, as some do, that the Nelson is a continuation of this river. Though in a sense it may be .argued that it is now a part of the Saskatchewan's system, the Nelson, as was mentioned before, is one of the survivors of Lake Agassiz.

The sources of the South Branch, which is sometimes considered a tributary of the North, are just as interesting as those of its partner and considerably more varied. The primary source is Bow Lake from which the Bow River pours so gaily down the pass through Banff to Calgary and beyond. Its confluence in southern Alberta with the Old Man, whose waters come from a number of mountain sources, is taken as the beginning of the South Saskatchewan proper. This was the great river of the buffalo plains in the early days, but because (unlike the North Branch) none of it passes through forest country after leaving the Rockies, it was never of great interest to the fur-traders. The South Branch was not prolific in amphibious animals. It flows easterly past Medicine Hat, then north-east across the provincial boundary where it gathers in the Red Deer, then up through the prairie past Saskatoon and Batoche to the Forks. The total length of the South Branch from Bow Lake to the Forks is 860 miles, the total drop to Lake Winnipeg about 600 feet. Bow Lake is one of the highest in the Rockies, and is still frozen in early June.

Between them the two branches of this river, together with their final run as a united stream, have a length just under 2,000 miles. Between them they embrace most of the farm land of Alberta and Saskatchewan.

Most easterners, I have discovered, have no idea how historic the Saskatchewan River is, much less that it was discovered only eight years after LaSalle explored the Mississippi to the Gulf. The "Kisiskatchewan", as the Indians called it, was first visited by the Hudson's Bay Company servant, Henry Kelsey, as early as 1690 and in the following year he penetrated some distance up the river from its mouth in Lake Winnipeg. Kelsey was therefore the first European to enter the Canadian prairie. He came in by way of the Nelson River from York Factory, and from that time on the Bay men believed that the river was essentially their territory. In 1741, one of the LaVérendrye parties explored the South Branch, and in

1774 Matthew Cocking and Samuel Hearne, the latter the greatest of the Bay Company's explorers, established a post on Cumberland Lake just west of The Pas. But many years previous to this, Canadians from Montreal were competing with the Bay on the Saskatchewan, and the feat of exploring and developing its trade was largely a Canadian one, some of the men being French, some of them English. It was here that the great rivalry between the Nor'-westers and the Bay men began.

"The Canadians are chosen Men inured to hardship & fatigue, under which your Present Servants would sink. A Man in the Canadian service who cannot carry two packs of eighty lbs each, one and one half leagues loses his Trip that is his Wages."

So wrote an officer of the Hudson's Bay Company from York Factory in a report to his superiors in England after seeing the feats on a Saskatchewan portage of a brigade of Canadians who had crossed the country from Montreal. The occasion of his report was probably a complaint from London that the number of pelts coming in from York Factory had been decreasing. The Bay men had little portage experience comparable to what the Canadians had, and at first did not use the tumplin, a leather band passed around the carrier's forehead in such a way that he controlled the weight by the muscles of the back and neck, and thus left his arms free and his body in balance as he walked.

Nor were the regular Nor'westers the only enemies of the Bay on the Saskatchewan in these early days. There was a French Canadian the Bay men called "Franceways", and they regarded him as a "pedlar", or poacher, because he worked on his own. The presence of this solitary trader in that empty region at so early a date has caused some fascinated conjecture. "Franceways" is of course an English version of "François", and Harold Innis deduced (a typical example of Innis' thoroughness as a scholar) that he was François Sassevillet, a canoeman mentioned in a licence granted to one Maurice Blondeau for Grand Portage in 1772.

"He is an ignorant old Frenchman," wrote Matthew Cocking in his journal. "I do not think he keeps a proper distance from his men, they coming into his apartment and talking with him as one of themselves. But what I am most surprised at, they keep no watch in the night; even when the Natives are lying in their plantation."

This quotation does much to explain the success of the Canadians against the Bay. For the English company was always, as one might expect, class-conscious, more conservative, more averse to going native than the Canadians. The reason why Franceways kept no watch was because he had no need to. The daughter of the local chief was his woman; he had married her *au façon du nord*, and his arrangement served the same purpose as the marriages of princes and princesses in the old countries of Europe. It cemented an alliance between Franceways and the Indians, and the result was that for a time the Frenchman was able to cut off two-thirds of the Saskatchewan River trade from the Honourable Company.

In *War and Peace* Tolstoy says that in historical events it is only unconscious activity that bears fruit, and that the man who plays a vital role in an historical drama never understands the final significance of his own acts. Though this theory may not work in the case of a Jefferson or a Churchill, it is magnificently applicable to the ironic history of Canada. It may sound strange to say that an illiterate *coureur de bois* like François was a maker of history, but he was. He and many of the other voyageurs knew nothing of history and cared less, but most of them were fully conscious that in their time and place they were privileged men. For they were free. They sprang from European peasants who had never been allowed to leave their villages or their lords' estates unless drafted into an army for a war they knew nothing about. But in the west of Canada they were their own masters and lived with the freedom of kings. In the Canadian service far more licence was granted to an independently minded voyageur than was ever given within the service of the Bay. That is why the Nor'-westers became such great explorers.

And now, at last, I come to that extraordinary character, Peter Pond, who was born in Connecticut and entered the fur trade after four campaigns in the Colonial wars.

Toward the end of his life, Peter Pond wrote a journal which has been thoroughly mined by historians. The pity is that there was not much more gold in the vein: the journal ends abruptly in mid-sentence with only a fraction recorded of an amazing life. As for its author, he died in poverty in 1807, an old man and forgotten, without anyone in his own time and place able to guess that his life's work would be remembered a century and a half later as having been vital to a nation then unborn.

It is constantly said of Peter Pond that he was an ignorant man. But was he? I know of nothing that can so close a man's mind to knowledge than the acceptance through life of the theories and

methods he learned at school and university. In the case of Peter
Pond the truth was the opposite. He spent his entire life in pursuit
of knowledge that his meagre schooling could never have given
him – knowledge through adventure, war, trade, unknown tribes
and lands, and above all, the knowledge that comes from learning
how to do new things. He was rough; he was probably very egotis-
tical. But the evidence that he was guilty of two separate murders
is so thin it can be discounted.

People have smiled patronizingly at the weird spelling in Pond's
narrative, noting that he could seldom spell accurately four suc-
cessive words. They forget that when Pond was a boy there was
no English dictionary available in Connecticut where he was born;
Samuel Johnson's *Dictionary Of The English Language* was published in London in Pond's sixteenth year. Before spelling was
standardized there could be such a variation that people almost
spelled as the fancy struck them. George Villiers, Duke of Buck-
ingham, has left behind him some dozen variants of his own sig-
nature!

When we remember this, we can learn more from the journal
of Peter Pond than historical facts; we can learn how people
talked in colonial New England in the middle eighteenth century.
For Pond's spelling is purely phonetic. If we read him aloud, we
hear in word after word the hard, broad accent of the English west
country from which most of the New England colonists had come:

"I was born in Milford in the countey of New Haven in Conn the
18 day of Jany 1740 and lived thare under the government and
protection of my parans til the year 56. A part of the British troops
which Ascaped at Bradixis Defeat on ye Bank of the Monagahaley
in Rea the french fortafycation which is now Cald fort Pitmen cam
to Milford. . . . Beaing then sixteen years of age I gave my Parans
to understand that I had a strong desire to be a Solge. That I was
determined to enlist under the Oficers that was Going from Milford & joine the army. But thay forbid me, and no wonder as my
father had a larg and young famerly I just begun to be of sum
youse to him in his afairs. Still the same Inklanation & Sperit
that my Ancestors Profest run thero my Vanes. It is well known
that from fifth Gineration downward we ware all Waryers Ither
by Sea or Land and in Dead so strong was the Propensatey for
the arme that I could not with stand its Temtations. One Eaveing
in April the Drams and Instraments of Musick ware all Imployed
to that Degrea that thay Charmed me. I repaird to a Publick

House whare Marth and Gollatrey was Highly Going on..." That night Pond joined what thereafter he always called "the Sarvis".

After fighting hard and well in the French and Indian Wars, seeing service under the command of Lord Jeffrey Amherst, Pond drifted into the fur trade and his first canoe was provided for him by no less a gentleman than James McGill. He went to Michilimackinac and thence to the Mississippi, where, at Portage du Chien, he saw traders "from eavery part of the Misseppey, even from Orleans." Returning to Michilimackinac in 1774, he found "a grate concors of people from all quorters." But when the American Revolution broke out, Pond had nothing to do with it. He returned to Montreal and made secure his place in the expanding North-west trade, and it was then that his great work of exploration began.

Entering the Saskatchewan River, Pond steadily examined its possibilities and laid the groundwork of the Company's food supply by discovering pemmican from the Indians and establishing a system of caching it along the banks, thus making the brigades much more independent than in the days when the men had to stop to fish or hunt. Along with Alexander Henry, Pond extended the fur trade into regions so remote from the St. Lawrence that at first the shipping of goods was a two seasons' job. He was the first white man to pass the Methye Portage into the Mackenzie basin; he was the first on the Athabaska. Now he had reached the point in the life of an active and original man when some inner force of which he may well be unconscious takes charge of him. Rough though he was, for him at this period all his past experience seems to have been an arch wherethrough gleamed "that untrav'lled world whose margins fade forever and forever as I move". He was after the Northwest Passage. In weather so cold his ink froze, he drew the first known map of the Northwest Territories. A later map he drew with the intention of presenting it to Catherine the Great of Russia when he reached her country after crossing the last of the countless horizons through which his life took him. Peter Pond's entire career, and especially the last part of it, lies solidly behind the famous final voyages of Mackenzie and Fraser.

Therefore this voyageur is a perfect illustration of Tolstoy's theory. Pond did not know — he could not have known at the time — that the treaty-makers in Versailles in 1783 had established the Canadian-American border with the express intent of making it impossible for Canada to survive. Their technique was to cut off the lines of communication from Montreal to the source of the one profitable trade the country had. But the treaty-makers knew nothing of the country west of Lake of the Woods, least of all that Pond, Alexander Henry and the Frobishers were moving west along the Saskatchewan, or that Pond himself had found a new trade area in the Athabaska. It was the Saskatchewan River which made possible an east-west lateral highway through Canada *above* the American border. Though the Athabaska trade, in the long run, was not adequate to save Canada economically, it gave the leaders of Canada hope at a moment when it was almost impossible for anyone to hope. It bridged a vital gap in the country's history, and when the country passed that gap later on, the northwest which Pond explored belonged to it.

In one way or another the Saskatchewan is associated with every name which became famous in the Canadian west. After Kelsey and the Vérendryes came Samuel Hearne, Peter Pangman, the brothers Frobisher, Alexander Henry and Pond himself; then Mackenzie, David Thompson, William McGillivray and Simon Fraser. In the nineteenth century it was at Batoche on the South Branch that Louis Riel and Gabriel Dumont stood with the tragic, nomadic race of *Métis* left behind on the plains by the matings of the voyageurs and their Indian women. It was toward the Saskatchewan that the militia of a united Canada marched to put down the Rebellion, and in the Saskatchewan territory that the Royal North West Mounted Police laid the groundwork of their reputation. Recently it was from a little town on the North Branch that John Diefenbaker flew into Ottawa with the biggest political majority in Canadian history.

"How can they?" I once heard an American woman say as she stared at the wind flattening the prairie grass beyond the Edmonton airport. "How can they *want* to live in a country like this?"

On winter days when forty-mile-an-hour gales tear across the prairie snows, this writer from gentle Nova Scotia has often had the same thought. There is no use in pretending that the Saskatchewan River country is a kind one to its people even now; half a century ago it was as cruel as the Pole. This is one of the sternest terrains I know inhabited by people living normal civilized lives. But the very fact that it *is* inhabited by civilized people has an historical significance most of us forget in these comfortable times.

If anyone wishes to know what life was like a century ago in Europe for the underprivileged — what life was like a full fifty years after the Selkirk Highlanders came to Manitoba — the best place to go is not to England, central Europe or even Montreal; it is to the Saskatchewan River country. Look at those millions of acres of sectional farms and the lonely little river towns where the farmers come in on Saturdays. Look at the early photographs of Saskatoon, which became a community only in 1882, and imagine yourself starting a life there at that time. Stand on the banks of the Saskatchewan and *feel* the river passing through that gigantic, lonely land, and then ask yourself what must have been in the minds of the first homesteaders who came west from settled Ontario, or who crossed the ocean and then travelled two-thirds of the way across Canada to *this*! I remember the feeling of fear it gave me as a boy when my mother told me of a relative who had gone to Saskatchewan from Nova Scotia, and how she had watched her son walking alone across the prairie to school until he became a tiny dot on the horizon.

In most ways, I have often thought, the courage of the homesteaders was greater than that of the voyageurs, for they had their families with them. How many fathers must have quailed at the responsibility they had assumed, at the results of their own ignorance, when all they could provide in the way of a house was a hole dug in the ground and roofed with sods! It is all very well to make jokes about the prairie that broke the plough so long as you make them in the east about certain glum novels of pioneering hardships. To make them in the west is like joking about rope in the house of the hanged man, for the hardships of this country are fresh in the memories of everyone over fifty. I have met a cultivated, brilliant woman in her fifties (her father was "county" in England) who spent her first year in Canada in a Saskatchewan sod hut.

It seems to me, since seeing the West, that the development of this Saskatchewan River country is an implicit refutation of all our sentimental images of the human past, for behind it was nothing more nor less than two basic needs which pre-twentieth-century society denied to everyone save a privileged few. Those needs were things the praisers of times past lack the experience — the experience, not the imagination — to comprehend: sufficient food, and sufficient freedom to raise your children, if not yourself, to the full stature of human beings. In Sutherlandshire little more than a century ago, after the lord's agents had burned the crofters out of their homes, they forbade them to eat the mussels on the shore because they were the lord's property. Thousands of the descendants of the evicted are on the plains of Saskatchewan today. Despair, no less than courage, is behind that province.

Or think how it was in middle and eastern Europe only a short while ago when whole families stampeded the immigrant ships. In Poland a century ago — perhaps more recently in backward regions — a landlord could possess a peasant girl merely by demanding her, and think himself magnanimous if he sent her family a sack of potatoes. Wars, press gangs and the lash lay behind many a homesteading family. Those who came to the United States may have believed the streets were paved with gold, but not one in a thousand who came to the Saskatchewan River country sought anything more than a home. If anyone were to ask me now what is the main common denominator which has held this nation together, I would answer very simply: a desire for a home, and a determination to keep it. *Ici, nous sommes chez nous* — the phrase is constantly used today in French Canada without sentimentality and without embarrassment.

The volume of effort expended by the Saskatchewan homesteaders can be estimated by looking at Saskatchewan life today and reflecting how quickly civilization has been established there. Drought and long distances, harsh winters and unpredictable rainfalls were always against the people. The deep trench of the river made it useless for water in dry seasons, yet civilization grew so fast it is hard for us to comprehend the advance. In the year when the Governors of the Hudson's Bay Company sold out their land rights in the West to the Canadian government, my own father was beginning school. Queen Victoria had been a widow for more than a decade when the Land Act was finally passed. Only twenty-two years before I myself was born — and as I write this I am fifty-three — Louis Riel and Gabriel Dumont made their last stand at Batoche. Only two years before I was born, Saskatchewan became a province.

All of this was possible because of the homesteaders and the driving need that took them there. Between 1876 and 1900 the silence of the prairie was split by the creaking of thousands of Red River carts as the families moved in: during that period some 88,000 entries were filed. In 1905 alone, spurred by Clifford Sifton's policy of opening the plains to "the man in the sheepskin coat with the broad wife", no less than 30,000 entries were made in the Saskatchewan country, and many of these newcomers knew no English. By that time the homestead acreage came close to the five million mark.

This would have signified little had the people been concerned only with wheat-growing. But not only did they crave an education, they craved a good one. Montreal had been settled for two centuries before it had a university, but the University of Saskatchewan was established five years after the land on which it stands had been incorporated within the province. A professor I met in Saskatoon only last year, originally a Nova Scotian and a man full of vigour still, told me of the morning when he and one or two colleagues saw their first students appear, and that the first subjects they taught them were Latin and Greek. Fifty years later the University of Saskatchewan was one of the best in the country.

"As for me and my house," Sinclair Ross quotes on the flyleaf of his novel of Saskatchewan in the depression years, "we will serve the Lord."

In the context of Sinclair Ross's story, this was not a pious quotation. A great bitterness lay behind it. The sufferings of the Saskatchewan people in the depression years when the dust storms blew, the memories of hardships which constantly renewed themselves, the narrowness of strict religions made all the more severe because people in little places cannot escape one another, the corrosions caused by aggression buried deep because they were too dangerous to release – all these elements were in Ross's novel of Saskatchewan. But endurance was also there, even endurance in religion. The God of tigers and lambs, of bacilli and penicillin, of drought and plenty had to be served. Otherwise the people would have perished.

These days when I visit Saskatchewan I remember how students from the farms starved during the depression years in order to get an education. I think how the people co-operated, and thereby upheld the dignity of their species. I feel that here I have made at least a brief acquaintance with the kind of unconscious force which Tolstoy believed is decisive in history. And flying home over the Saskatchewan River, sometimes I have felt I could almost see those ghostly canoe brigades, tiny in that vast and tawny setting, paddling firmly upward against the current of the stream.

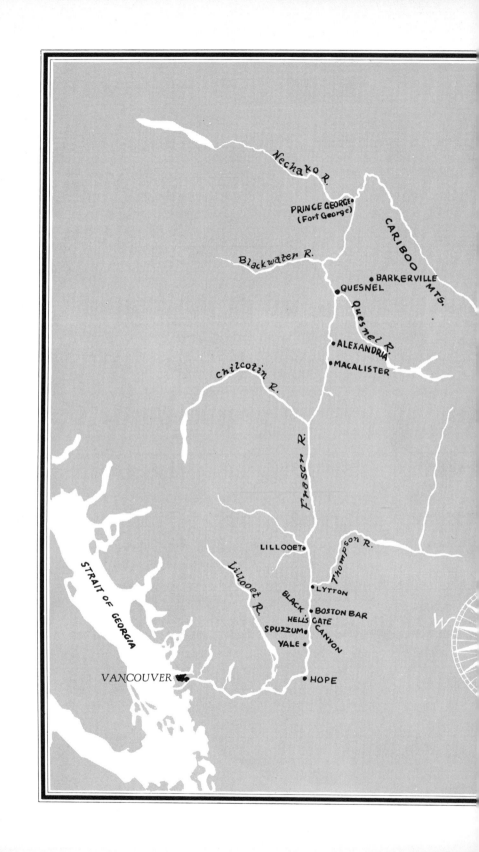

The Fraser

The Fraser was the end of the route. Here occurred the climax of two centuries of canoe exploration in North America.

No easterner, least of all one from the Maritime Provinces, is ever likely to feel at home beside the Fraser River. It is alien to everything he knows, and so is its land. Great men have passed through its story, but they did not grow out of the country on which, for brief moments, they partially imposed their wills. Wild and amazing experiences have been recorded in some of the little towns along the Black Canyon and up tributaries like the Thompson, the Lillooet and the Quesnel, but some of these towns are ghosts today and the decendants of the men who once thronged and brawled in them live elsewhere. It took the people of Switzerland many centuries to establish a real human relationship with the Alps. It will take Canadians of the scientific age at least half as long to do the same with the Rocky Mountains.

This is the most exciting country in Canada, and I don't see how anyone could visit any part of it without longing to return. Its beauty makes you catch your breath. But it was a westerner, Bruce Hutchison, who remarked that the beauty of the most spectacular parts of the

MT. ROBSON

Fraser River is that of a nightmare. This is the savagest of all the major rivers of America. It is probably the savagest in the world.

The Fraser is a mountain system, and though the area of its drainage basin is little more than 90,000 miles, here the figures are deceptively low because northern mountains catch huge quantities of snow, especially if they are close to an ocean like the Pacific. The Fraser's total length is 850 miles, its course the shape of the letter S drawn by a man in *delirium tremens*. It rises at 52° 45′ north latitude in two small branches fed by Mount Robson's glacier just west of the Divide, and the moment these feeder streams unite, they find a course in which to run. There in the absolute wilderness of the northern Rockies the drama of the Fraser begins.

Though the ultimate destination lies hundreds of miles to the south-west, the Fraser begins its career by charging north-west in a wide, wavering curve along the Rocky Mountain Trench. After about two hundred miles the rushing waters encounter the northern spur of the Cariboo Mountains, they sweep in a fierce arc around them, then they plunge directly south. Twisting furiously, with only a few brief interludes of relative calm, the Fraser roars for four hundred miles down to the little town of Hope, which began its existence as a Hudson's Bay Company post and was well named, as so many of these posts were, when one considers what awaited a traveller going north before the roads were built. At Hope the Fraser at last breaks out of its mountain trap.

To the geographer what happens here is one of the most exciting natural spectacles in Canada. Within a distance of a mile the entire character of the river changes and this tyrannosaurus of a stream turns sweet and gentle. In a broad valley shining in the sun, with a width the same as the St. John's below Fredericton, the Fraser winds calmly through the loveliest farming valley in the land. The air is balmy, the cattle as sleek as in a Cambridgeshire meadow, the snow peaks Olympian in the safe distance. During these last eighty miles the river traverses most of human British Columbia, for it is in this beautiful corner, and in the twin cities at the estuary, that the bulk of British Columbians live. At the end of its course the Fraser is old King Lear with the rage gone. But before the ocean swallows it, receiving its water through a surprisingly small delta, the river makes one final assertion of its true character. For miles it stains the clean brine of Georgia

Strait with the dirty yellow silt it has torn out of the mountains all the way from the top of the Cariboo to the Canyon's end at Hope.

"If a river could flow on the moon," I thought as I flew over the Black Canyon, "it would probably look like this."

The idea is not so far-fetched as it looks, because from twenty thousand feet a lot of the land around the central Fraser seems just as chaotic and devoid of purpose as the moon's surface seen through a telescope. Those peaks which inspire you when you stare at them from the ground are harsh, barren ridges of rock where nothing lives. The valleys where the elk browse and the little streams cascade are cruel scars. From the air the Rocky Mountains are seldom beautiful.

Yet the air is the best place to study the Fraser if you wish to understand the logic of its course. On the ground, travelling that fantastic highway which has grown out of the old Cariboo Road, the river seems to be coming at you from all directions and the road beside it twists like a spiral stair so that on a dull day, without the sun to tell you your course, you often don't know whether you are travelling north or south. But from the air the twists in the river are seen to be perfectly logical.

The necessity of every river is to get down to sea level by the shortest route possible, and this may vary from a gentle winding in a set direction to a tortured course through every point of the compass until the goal has been reached. The Fraser's terrain is the toughest of any major river in America, possibly of any in the world, and so is its problem.

From the air you see how it solves it. As all of its course save the final eighty miles lies in a mountain labyrinth where the peaks and ranges literally jostle one another, the Fraser must outflank ridge after ridge, and in some places bore its way through sheer walls of rock. From the air you see it like a very yellow, very thin snake that looks as if it had died after having had a convulsion in a rock trap. From the air there is no life in the Fraser, and it does not look like a river at all.

On the ground it explodes with life, and there is a marvellous variety in the spectacle through which it flows. Here the colours are so bold and strong — sage green, orange of sandstone, viridian of hemlock and fir, blue of translucent skies, Wimbledon green on the rare benches where the cattle graze — that a visitor from the east feels he has been translated into a larger, brighter, more exciting existence. The wild flowers are lovely along the Fraser, the wind sounds as though the mountains were breathing, the dawns and sunsets are such that you can only stare at them in silent wonder. Then you look down the steep trench — in many places you look down thousands of feet — and you see the intruder. That furious, frothing water scandalously yellow against the green — where did it come from and how did it get here?

This savage thing! On all the major rivers you expect the occasional turbulence, and you assume that all mountain streams are cataracts. Rivers like the St. Lawrence quickly calm down after their rapids, and mountain streams like the Kicking Horse are shallow and short. But the Fraser is neither short nor shallow. It is nearly a hundred miles longer than the Rhine, and it flows with cataract force for more than six hundred miles with only a few interludes of relative quiet. In a sense the Fraser does not flow at all: it seethes along with whirlpools so fierce that a log going down it may circle the same spot for days as though caught in a liquid merry-go-round. It roars like an ocean in storm, but ocean storms blow themselves out while the Fraser's roar is forever.

This is the most remorseless force of nature in Canada, and its effect on the person who travels beside it is curious. As you drive north in your car you twist for hour after hour around one hairpin bend after another. Some of these curves around abutments of the cliff can turn the knees of a height-shy traveller to water and I, personally, am glad I was able to travel from Lytton to Lillooet before the road was improved to the width of a super-highway. Past Yale, past Spuzzum and Boston Bar, up through Lytton to Lillooet that curving highway took us, sometimes through little tunnels in the cliff itself, once or twice around a narrow bend with an unguarded edge and a drop thousands of feet straight down — the road is almost as exciting as the river itself, and you remember that in some of these towns, now quiet and half alive, thousands of desperate men once lived as dangerously as soldiers in war when they panned this river for gold. A little beyond Lytton the road leaves the river, and if you wish to follow the water you must abandon your car and take to the Pacific Great Eastern Railway. Miles higher up to the north, the road and river re-join at Macalister.

All this time and all these miles the Fraser has been working on you. Sometimes you are so close to the water that its yellow malevolence boils into your subconscious, but most of the time you are so high that it looks as static as it does from the air. Almost never does it seem to belong where it is. Yet it is there, and after you have spent several days beside it, the Fraser intrudes into yourself also, and you are apt to see it in your sleep.

The Fraser River, which seems absolutely hostile to man and all his works, has been as important to British Columbia as the St. Lawrence has been to Quebec. This is another of the amazing facts about it. In his book on the river, Bruce Hutchison argues that the Fraser has practically created the province. So, in a sense, it has, and in a manner awe-inspiring to people from quieter regions.

Fraser salmon, which supported an Indian culture long before the white man came, today gives British Columbia a richer fishing industry than that of the three Maritime Provinces combined. The life-cycle of the Sockeye salmon is one of those natural dramas so suggestive that the very symbolism of it cuts too close to the human knuckle for mental comfort. The story of the salmon's fight up the river to spawn and die has been told so often and well that I will not repeat it here. Everyone — at least everyone in British Columbia — knows about the fish ladders at Hell's Gate, about the river visibly bulging with life when the big runs come in, about the tributaries turning blood-red as the fish expire while giving life to a new generation, about the bears that wade into the shallows to eat them, about the males fighting with each other for the privilege of dying beside the females of their choice, about the stench which pollutes the wilderness when the bodies decompose. In the upper reaches the salmon are often too far gone in the death process to be eaten by humans, and the great catches are made in the sea when the fish are bright and strong swimming in toward the estuary, or in the lowermost reaches near Mission before the final death-rush begins.

Fraser gold, discovered in 1856 or 1857 (the exact date is uncertain) caused an epic of suffering worse even than the record of the Klondike. Terrible though the Chilkoot was, it was not so cruel as the Fraser rapids down which those heroic fools tried to flounder on rafts. The amount of gold taken out of the sand-bars and lodes at Yale, Boston Bar, Barkerville and up the Thompson and Lillooet was trivial compared to the hardship and heroism that paid for it, nor were the individual fortunes more permanent than gold-rush fortunes anywhere else. This story is also too familiar to bear repetition.

But the Fraser gold had two by-products of infinite importance to British Columbia. The river in the end carried thousands of disappointed miners down to the estuary where they were deposited like so much sediment with neither the will nor the means to return. Many stayed permanently, and added themselves to the nucleus of humanity which built Vancouver into our third city within three generations. The second by-product was the Cariboo Road.

In 1861 Governor James Douglas, one of the most dynamic men in Canadian history, realized that unless help on a huge scale were provided for the obsessed lunatics digging and panning up the Fraser Canyon, thousands of them would die of famine and cold. He therefore ordered his Royal Engineers to build a route into the interior, and the result was the most spectacularly dangerous highway in America. When the Engineers finished their work, the Cariboo Road was a ledge in the cliff sides three hundred and eighty-five miles long and eighteen feet wide. In places the drop from the unguarded lip was thousands of feet, and many a horse and mule, and quite a few men also, hurtled off and down to the end of their troubles. One imaginative teamster even introduced camels to the Cariboo, thinking they would be more sure-footed than horses and mules, but their smell so frightened the other pack animals that the camels were taken off the road.

So far as the original stampeders were concerned, this famous road probably did more harm than good: it provided an excuse for thousands more to join the hordes of gold-fevered men already working there. But when the stampede petered out and the hurdy-gurdy girls and the chisellers went south, when the roaring shack towns turned into bleaching ghost towns, the road was there and remained. It led saner men into the interior who built logging camps and established the great ranches which make British Columbia's Dry Belt a rival in stock raising to the American southwest.

Fraser silt, deposited over millenniums in the delta and in the valley behind New Westminster, enabled the growing population of the Canadian west coast first to feed itself and later to develop an agricultural exporting industry. Acre for acre, the arable land of the lower Fraser Valley is among the richest in Canada.

The economic development forced on the province by the Fraser led inevitably to the construction of railways, and here again the river turned out to be the key to a tremendous engineering problem. The two transcontinental lines, after threading the Rockies from the Kicking Horse and the Yellowhead, use the Canyon for their final runs into Vancouver. And the Pacific Great Eastern, the most exciting railway this side of Switzerland, swaying at dizzy heights along the cliffs, goes north to Prince George and finally links the Pacific Coast to the Peace River country.

The world knows little of the Fraser's history – nor does eastern Canada, for that matter – and I would guess there are two reasons for this ignorance. In the first place, nobody can imagine what the river is like unless he has seen it with his own eyes, for there is nothing else resembling it on this continent, and I doubt if there is anything else resembling it in the world. In the second place, modern people everywhere have been conditioned to think of post-voyageur explorations and settlements in the far west in the patterns established in the United States. From Francis Parkman's *The Oregon Trail* to the latest covered-wagon television show, the American story has been told and re-told countless times. The story of British Columbia's exploration and settlement has hardly been heard at all.

It was quite different owing to the tradition of Canadian exploration and the nature of the British Columbian terrain. Though the passes through the American Rockies are sometimes difficult, horses and mules could usually negotiate them. But there is nothing in the American west like the nightmare of the Fraser Canyon. Before the building of the Cariboo Road, the pioneers of British Columbia still had to depend on the canoe or on boats, and use them on a river which no human being in his senses would try to navigate unless he had to. Later, when they built roads, they had to blast them out of sheer cliffs.

Incredibly, steamboats were used for a time in the Canyon itself, and this fact alone points up the harshness of the Canadian experience in the early days of the coastal province. If anyone stands on the road above Hell's Gate – better still, if he descends to the edge of the river itself at that point – he finds it impossible to believe that anyone would even try to drive a steamboat up-river against that ferocious torrent. But as the alternative was back-breaking labour, men not only tried, they actually succeeded in using steamboats for a while. They dragged them up by means of winches on the ships with hundreds of men heaving on cables as they toiled along the ledges above the water. Many of the men on the ropes were Chinese, and perhaps some of them had worked

on the Yangtse or the Yellow River in their native land. The ships'
engines roared, sometimes the boilers exploded from excess of
pressure, but they were hauled up the canyon against that cataract.

The pioneers of British Columbia, and later the technicians
and engineers, circumvented the river's obstacles even though
they could not tame the river itself. The challenges they met were
never adequately described by them, nor do I think that anyone
now can tell their story as it truly was. But to some extent we can
guess at it by acquainting ourselves with the river itself, and by
looking at some of its vital facts.

The mountains through which the Fraser finds or carves a path
are far from the world's highest, but they cover a huge area and
are extremely varied. For miles above Lytton the river passes
through the so-called Dry Belt of British Columbia where the traveller is astonished to encounter the sage brush, tumbleweed and
county-sized ranches associated with the American south-west,
and is warned against rattlesnakes on rocky trails. Little rain falls
here, and if all the Fraser's course lay through country like this,
its volume of flow would be moderate. But all of its course does not
lie through country like this.

Many of the ranges sloping in chaos in the general direction of
the Fraser are exposed to moist Pacific winds, and in winter they
collect billions of tons of snow. By mid-June most of this snow has
turned into water and the water runs. The Fraser, draining an
area of 91,600 square miles, has to carry all this run-off to the sea.
A geographer once told me that the mere statement of these facts
tells you all you need to know about the nature of the river. It does,
I suppose, to a man with a geographer's imagination. But I myself
had to see it to believe it.

"When you reach Lytton," a British Columbian told me in Montreal, "be sure to stand on that little bridge where the Thompson
enters. It's a wonderful sight. Thompson water is blue-green and
Fraser water is yellow gumbo. You can see them both together —
two separate streams in the same course."

I thought I understood what he meant, for the year previous I
had been on the Mackenzie and seen the phenomenon of the
Liard's brown water flowing along the left bank while the clean
Mackenzie water keeps to the right. The two streams are distin-
guishable side by side for nearly two hundred miles below Fort

Simpson. It takes the Mackenzie, one of the most powerful streams in the land, all this distance to absorb its chief tributary.

When I stood on the Lytton bridge the sight was indeed wonderful, but it bore no resemblance to anything I had expected. The Thompson is the Fraser's chief tributary, a major stream in its own right, a mountain stream also, and it does not so much enter the Fraser as smash its way into it like a liquid battering ram. From the bridge I saw its water plunging into the Fraser just as the man said, blue-green into the Fraser's yellow froth. Then it completely disappeared. The Fraser swallows the Thompson in less than a hundred yards!

As soon as you pass beyond Lytton on the way up-river, you see evidence of the Fraser's power in what it has done to the land. Above Lillooet it has carved out a minor Grand Canyon. Farther up in the plateaus of the ranching country it is almost subterranean: you travel for miles across the ranges and think no water is anywhere and then suddenly you come to the trench and stare far, far down and there is that infernal yellow line frothing along.

But it is at Hell's Gate, its passage made still more narrow by rock-falls from railway blasting, that the prolonged violence of the river reaches its climax, and the best way I can think of describing its ferocity here is by making some comparisons with the St. Lawrence.

The mean flow of the St. Lawrence is 543,000 cubic feet per second, the Fraser's 92,600. But the width of the St. Lawrence in the Seaways section where the Victoria Bridge crosses to Montreal, *before* it has received the Richelieu, the St. Maurice or any substantial weight of the Ottawa, is more than a mile and a half. The width of the Fraser at Hell's Gate, *after* it has received the Nechako, the Blackwater, the Chilcotin, the Quesnel, the Lillooet, the Thompson and nearly all its less famous tributaries, is hardly more than fifty yards! This means that on an average day a first-class fisherman can cast a line across a river carrying one-fifth the flow of the St. Lawrence!

But there are days on the Fraser which are not average, days which come after steady sunshine and a succession of warm nights have melted the mountain snows in a rush. Then the Fraser becomes incredible.

During the flood of 1948 a flow of 543,000 cubic feet per second was recorded on the Fraser; in the worse flood of 1894, the flow was estimated at 600,000 cubic feet per second. In other words, there was at least one recorded occasion when 57,000 more cubic feet of water per second went through the gap at Hell's Gate than passes on an average day between Quebec and Lévis!

What this meant to the gentle valley below Hope amounted on both occasions to a national catastrophe. Thousands of acres were awash, barns and houses were carried away, cattle were drowned and the bodies of cows were seen floating in the yellow smear spread for miles into the Strait of Georgia. But in the Black Canyon little was changed because its walls are so sheer and its trough so deep it could hold all the rivers of North America without overflowing. In the twisted gorge the Fraser boiled and roared at prodigious depths and at velocities exceeding twenty knots. It churned millions of tons of sand in its whirlpools, its backwashes tossed giant logs like splinters end over end, it killed thousands of salmon by exhausting the life out of them or by hurling them clear of the water against rocks which broke their spines. It wore several more inches off the little islands which survive in the channel shaped like the pre-Dreadnaught battleships of the German Kaiser's High Seas Fleet.

I was not on the Fraser when these violent events occurred, but if I had flown over the Canyon at those times, I would have seen nothing out of the ordinary at ten thousand feet.

This river was navigated — at least most of it was — by human beings in canoes of the North West Company, and of all the facts connected with the Fraser, this single one is the most impressive to anyone who knows the region. It was later navigated — if you can apply such a technical word to an insanely ignorant venture — by a few stampeders who built themselves rafts intending to float down the current, found themselves trapped in the Canyon and clung to the rafts because this was all they could do. But no stampeder truly navigated the Fraser any more than the logs do. Nor, for that matter, did the Frenchman who swam the river in 1958 swim it in the sense that experts swim the English Channel or Lake Ontario. Equipped with a frogman's outfit, he also was carried down like a log.

But voyageurs legitimately navigated nearly all of it. First, Alexander Mackenzie entered its upper waters in 1793 when he cut through the mountains by way of the Peace on the journey which led him to Dean Channel and the coast. When he launched his canoe on the western side of the Divide he was not sure where the river would lead him, but he soon discovered that this was the worst river in his experience. His canoe was wrecked in the upper Canyon by Fort George and he and his men were nearly drowned. They patched their canoe and continued, but at the point now called Alexandria, Mackenzie decided he had had enough. Besides being a magnificent river man, he had a poet's intuition: he abandoned the river in the nick of time and went overland to the Bella Coola. A few more miles and he would have passed the point of no return.

Fifteen years later in 1808 a different type of Scot, the stolid, factual Simon Fraser, following in the path of the man he referred to tauntingly in his journal as "Sir A. M. K." (the explorer's jealousy again), passed the point where Mackenzie left the river and kept on going. Like Mackenzie before him, Fraser also was ignorant of the river's nature and even of what river it was. He believed it was the Columbia, and he had entered it with the specific mission of exploring it to the mouth in order to establish British rights to the entire Columbia region. When he entered the Black Canyon and the waters whirled him, he knew he must go through or perish. The result was the climax of the long story of the fur-trading voyages which began when Etienne Brûlé went up the Ottawa to the Chaudière Falls. Simon Fraser's was the most terrible and wonderful inland voyage in the history of North America.

Tiny in their birch-bark canoes, the voyageurs stared up thousands of feet at the walls of that canyon. The river roared so loud they could not hear each other speak, it twisted so fast they could not prepare themselves for what lay around the next bend. When they watched the walls of the canyon flashing past, they must have realized that no canoe, for that matter no ship hitherto built, had ever travelled for such a length of time at such a speed and survived. They were spun like tops in the whirlpools, and when backwashes swept them ashore, they portaged over cliffs thousands of feet high, for they could not survive if they stayed still – their food was running out – and they did not believe it possible to return. Finally they reached Hell's Gate, and here their experience inspired the most celebrated passage in Fraser's Journal:

"I have been for a long period in the Rocky Mountains, but have never seen anything like this country. It is so wild I cannot find words to describe it at times. We had to pass where no human being should venture; yet in those places there is a regular pathway impressed, or rather indented on the very rocks by frequent travelling."

This so-called pathway had been made by Indians who had been in the region so long that the village now called Lytton claims to be the oldest permanently settled place in North America. Fraser and his men, their canoes abandoned on the shore, crawled sideways with their packs along the cliff, hanging on to twisted vines "formed like a ladder or the shrouds of a ship". Somehow they got through, and lower down they bought Indian dugouts and so reached the ocean.

It was typical of Simon Fraser that when he reached the delta he was as disappointed as Mackenzie had been when he came to the larger delta on the Beaufort Sea. Whatever else this awful river might be, Fraser knew it was not the Columbia. Not being able to foresee the future, he assumed that his mission was a failure and turned back.

The return journey was in some ways worse than the passage going down, though at least its dangers could no longer surprise them. The Indians turned hostile and bombarded them with rocks which they dropped from the cliffs above. Their supplies were nearly gone, their clothing in rags, their shoes holed and torn, their bodies exhausted and their minds dazed with hardship and danger. Simon Fraser was not an especially attractive character, but his dogged courage was rock-like, and his powers of leadership must surely have been as great as Mackenzie's. At the moment of their bottom despair, this normally undramatic man made his Scottish and *Canadien* voyageurs join hands and take this oath: "I solemnly swear before Almighty God that I shall sooner perish than forsake any of our crew during the present voyage."

They got through. On the northern end of Hell's Gate they found their abandoned canoes intact, and those amazing men dragged and paddled them north the way they had come. They reached Fort George in thirty-four days. This last statement should be repeated: Simon Fraser and his party, fighting their way back against that river, reached Fort George in thirty-four days!

While this voyage was taking place, the North West Company's geographer, David Thompson, was on the river which Fraser had at first believed he was on himself, and three years later Thompson explored the Columbia to its mouth.

Out of Fraser's voyage grew the story of British Columbia, which unfolded so rapidly in the next one hundred and fifty years that British Columbians themselves seem unable to realize how astonishing their advance has been. It took generations for eastern cities like Quebec and Halifax to grow, but Vancouver and the little towns of the lower Fraser Valley leaped up in a moment of time. As late as the First World War, the sole university in the province was little more than an extension department of McGill; today it is larger than McGill and one of the best institutions in the country. Vancouver is now Canada's third city; a century hence it will probably be her first, as the Pacific replaces the Atlantic in human importance.

But progress, not even with all the instruments of a growing science behind it, will never change the character of British Columbia's chief river. It will always be possible to see much of it as it appeared to the voyageurs, and it will never be possible to tame it. So long as mountain snows melt, the Fraser will roar and foam, for even if the Black Canyon were walled off, the water would find or make another one, and the Fraser would still be the narrowest and most savage of all the major rivers of this continent.

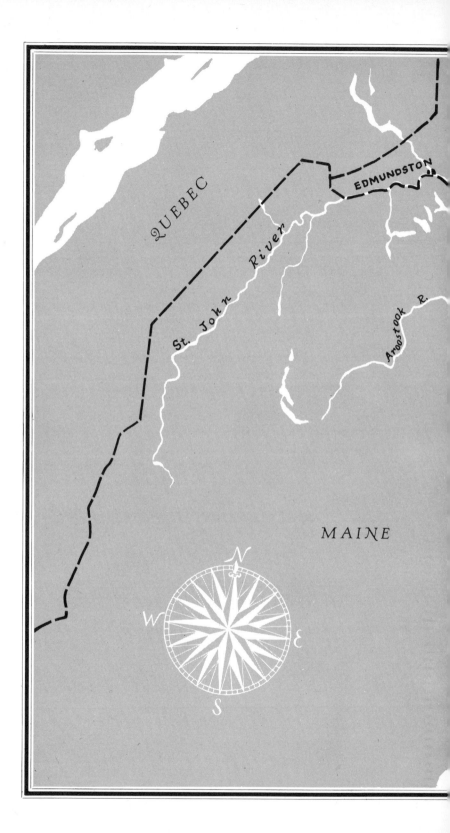

The St. John

LEONARD

GRAND
•FALLS

St. River

Tobique R.

ROOSTOOK

NEW BRUNSWICK

• BEECHWOOD

Nashwaak R.

• WOODSTOCK

River

•MARYSVILLE

FREDERICTON•

OROMOCTO ISLAND

•MAUGERVILLE

OROMOCTO•

Oromocto R.

Jemseg R.

GRAND LAKE

•GAGETOWN

Kennebecasis R.

LONG REACH

• ROTHESAY

GRAND BAY •

SAINT JOHN

REVERSIBLE FALLS

BAY OF FUNDY

The St. John

For myself, a return to the St. John River is like a homecoming. Deep and splendid though the river is, it is not like any of the others of the country which we Maritimers, in my grandfather's day, referred to as "Canada". The old Maritime Provinces have changed less than any part of North America. What they have lost in prosperity, they have gained in coherence, and on the whole the life there is the quietest and happiest in the country. Everything here is on a small scale easily comprehended, close to the English or Scottish past of the people, and the whole region still abounds in the eccentric characters which only small old places, sure of themselves emotionally, seem able to afford.

Years ago I heard one of those Maritime Province stories which nobody verifies for fear it will turn out to be false. On a tributary of the St. John River, around the turn of the century, quite a few lumbermen were owners of dress suits with all the fixings: boiled shirts, starched wing collars, white ties and gloves, black silk socks and patent leather pumps. They had acquired this apparel from a man they respected as the best fly-fisherman, the best bird-shot and the best still-hunter they knew in a district where standards in these activities were high. He was an Englishman and a remittance man, and each year his family had his former tailor and haberdasher send him the kind of garments they presumed he required in the St. John River country. The remittance man, who lived in a shack and wore nothing but work clothes, passed on the parcels to his friends. He spoke little about himself, but whenever anyone asked him why he had chosen to live there, his answer was always the same.

"One lives like a gentleman here. One has all the fishing and shooting one wants at one's door. This is a happy land."

I hope the story is even half-true, for happiness is the word which always comes to my mind when I think of the River St. John. It is the shortest of our principal streams, being only about 420 miles long, and its system is a small one. Yet it offers so much variety of scenery that a stranger travelling along it encounters a surprise every twenty miles or so. The St. John is intimate and very beautiful. On fine summer days the colours in its lower reaches shift from ocean blue to delphinium blue to a deep quivering violet according to the intensity of the light given out by the sky. A sudden rain in the Aroostook country can make the upper St. John look as brown as the Red while the lower stream is still clear, and indeed the depth lower down is so great, the current so gentle, that the silt from the upper river tends to sink to the bottom, with the result that the water of the lower St. John is beautifully clear most of the time. Sunsets in the Long Reach are as majestic as sunsets in a deep fjord of Norway. At dawn and in the evening some of the settled sections have pastel hues soft as in southern England. "Tenderly, day that I have loved, I close your eyes" — I thought of this line of Rupert Brooke the last time I heard the bells of Fredericton chime across the stream after sunset.

The happiness associated with the St. John, especially in the older communities lower down the river, is of a kind the world is losing everywhere. It proceeds from a life closely entwined with the river and with woods which are still wild and abundant with game: with family farms, small towns, neighbourly villages and plain people living with nature at their doors and not much troubled by ambition. Most of the intensely ambitious Maritimers emigrate; most of those who remain regard the living of a good life as more important than the using of a life for the sake of achievement. The St. John River country is old-fashioned; it makes you think of the growing years of eastern America before the pressures developed.

There are several reasons for this. Not only is New Brunswick a geographical offshoot of New England; the people inhabiting the St. John Valley from Woodstock to the Reversible Falls are nearly all descended from the original Anglo-Saxon stock which pioneered the United States. After the first tentative French occupation petered out, the Loyalists came to the Valley at the end of the eighteenth century and settled it. With them they brought, along with a reinforced loyalty to the Crown, most of the habits, virtues and limitations acquired by their ancestors in the first century and a half of the English-American experience. But because they were a twice-transplanted people, the lower St. John is much younger in terms of settlement than Massachusetts or New York, and from the visual standpoint this has been a calamity. The old New England towns were built in the most exquisite period of domestic architecture ever known, but most of the St. John River towns suffer from the bad taste of the nineteenth century with its ugly angles and harsh red brick. But their way of life is not reflected in their buildings. It still belongs to an earlier period than survives in any place I know in the northern states of the American east.

"I come to Canada regularly," a retired American general said to me, "because it reminds me so much of home when I was a boy. I can close my eyes and hear the old folks talk."

The St. John River people along the lower reaches are such staunch retainers of the past that "conservative" is too weak a word to apply to them. There is something endearing in their stubborn dislike of change. There can be something paradoxical about it, too.

Few Canadians have contributed more to the speed of modern living than Rupert Turnbull, who invented the variable-pitch propeller, built the first wind tunnel in Canada and was the first man to close the wing in aircraft. Although for a time he did research under Edison in Menlo Park, for most of his career Turnbull worked in his private laboratory at Rothesay where the Kennebecasis comes in to share Grand Bay with the St. John. In his personal life this singular inventor was so averse to change that he lived like a country squire of the last century. He sailed, he fished, he shot ducks into his early eighties. He disliked speed, and when he reluctantly bought an automobile, he never drove it faster than twenty-five miles an hour. When New Brunswick in the early 1920s grudgingly changed the rule of the road from left to right (in other words, from English to American) he so disapproved of the alteration that he tried to ignore it. Finding progress difficult with the traffic coming from the opposite direction, he at last accepted a compromise. Instead of driving on the left hand side of the road, he drove in the middle, and in a region full of individualists, he was not only condoned, he was applauded.

For years this conservatism of the St. John River country, until recently the heart of New Brunswick province, was responsible for the fact that New Brunswick had one of the lowest average income figures per capita in the whole country. Power plants came late to the St. John. Though the river has a great weight of water and the most spectacular cataract east of Montmorency, it was 1925 before a power plant was opened at Grand Falls. This plant, together with the development of the pulp and paper industry higher up at Edmundston, changed the economy of the upper stream, and also made its appearance much less attractive. To this day there are people living lower down the river who regret that a pleasant village like the old Grand Falls should have been converted into a factory town with wide streets and a movie house. It was not until 1950 that engineers undertook an exhaustive survey of the St. John River basin in search of power sources for a province finally forced to admit that it was suffering the fate of all raw producers in the technological age, and it was only in 1958 that the dam at Beechwood came into operation. The engineers installed fish ladders for the salmon swimming up to the spawning beds on the Tobique, but salmon cannot so easily be guided back the same way, and a great number of fingerlings are sure to perish in the turbines. Knowing the region pretty well, and knowing the Maritime Province mentality since childhood, I was not surprised to encounter a good many negative opinions about the Beechwood dam just after it came into operation.

"What's the use of installing new manufactures here?" said one man. "I'd like to ask you what good *that* is going to do New Brunswick. The rest of the country has fixed the freight rates against the Maritimes, so even if the dam does anything — and it probably won't — what difference will it make to us? We'll still be outsold one way or the other."

And another said: "This was the most beautiful salmon river on the whole Atlantic seaboard of America. Then some engineers come along and ruin it."

And another: "Do you really want to know why they built that dam? For precisely the same reason the Egyptians and the Burmese and Ghanaians want to build dams where dams never were. It's become a status-symbol for this crazy modern world that knows how to do anything else except be sensible and happy. That dam isn't worth an hour's fishing."

The St. John River people can at times be vague about their first New Brunswick ancestors — not *very* vague, but vague because their ancestors, when they think of them at all, seem so much like themselves today that there is no point in talking about them. The ancestors of nearly all of them were United Empire Loyalists, many of them soldiers in King George's American regiments during the Revolutionary War. Their present descendants have inherited their conservatism. They do not dislike Americans — how can they, being in some senses more authentically Ameri-

can than most American citizens of the present? They admit the
United States has been as successful as Mr. Jefferson hoped she
would be, but at the same time they feel that the price of success
has been too high. With the pride of the unappreciated they accept it as a compliment when bustling moderns of a city like
Toronto accuse them of lack of enterprise. They are proud of the
simple dignity of their own past, and of the dignity of this river
they have so carefully preserved. The American general knew
what he was talking about when he said that the country-dwelling
Loyalist is a survival of the old American society.

Sometimes I amuse myself by imagining the feelings of famous
Americans of past eras if these same Americans were reincar-
nated into the present. What would Longfellow say of the motels,
beach cabins, billboards and roadside eating stands of Maine's
U.S. 1? Emerson in modern Boston, Whittier in Peyton Place —
the thought of these grave old Americans in the society which developed after them fills the one-eighth of me which is Loyalist
with a quiet amusement. Pre-industrial New England smelled of
harbours with rope walks and caulking irons, of kitchens warm
with fresh bread, of root cellars and October leaves and crab-apple
jelly and scrubbed churches where incense never burned. Many
places in the St. John River country still do. At Market Slip in
Saint John City, Longfellow could still discover the beauty and
mystery of ships as they were before ships turned into a combina-
tion of huge machines and floating Grand Hotels. Fredericton
today is not unlike Emerson's Concord, though the equivalents of
State Street and Washington Street are here called Queen Street
and Regent Street. In Maugerville (pronounced "Majorville")
there must still be a few of Whittier's barefoot boys. All along the
lower St. John from Woodstock to the mouth are people bearing
names well known in colonial America. Nearly all the Winslows
who were descended from the only Pilgrim Father to have his
picture painted have disappeared in the United States after a
long record of service in which one of them was Admiral of the
United States Pacific fleet. But along the St. John River today
there are quite a few Winslows living there simply.

This is a wonderful country for growing boys, as was the old
New England of chores and fishing and rural schools. Here a
growing boy can live close to nature and at the same time see
an integrated society reduced to a boy's scale. Until recently it was
like this all along the St. John, and in some places it still is. No

wonder so many Maritime Province boys, grown into successful men in the large cities, sigh for home as the grown Adam sighed for the Garden. They had good childhoods there. Their selective memories have censored out the bad spots and the dull spots and have created the kind of poetry which Stephen Leacock, raised in a rawer community composed of the same stock, wove into his *Sunshine Sketches of a Little Town.*

The lure of this land to the expatriate is as strong as the invisible thread of Chesterton's Father Brown which could draw a man home from the remotest corner of the world. It is like the mysterious pull of the spawning beds to the Atlantic salmon, which do not die after spawning as the Pacific salmon do. Lord Beaverbrook, to judge from anecdotes and his own stories, never found in London the inner satisfaction he knew in his New Brunswick boyhood. To a Maritimer there is something charming in the provincial arrogance which caused this tough and difficult man, during a war-time conference with Roosevelt, Churchill and Stalin, to force the great men to learn the old New Brunswick lumbering song about the Jones boys' sawmill. There is something touching in the salmon-like returns of this formidable old egotist to his native land, in his desire to make Englishmen admit that it is a wonderful place. But if I know the St. John River mentality, I suspect that they have always assumed, without having to mention it except to strangers, that Lord Beaverbrook is not quite one of them, having been raised on the Miramichi in a different part of the province. It would not surprise me if Lord Beaverbrook has not encountered with familiar exasperation the built-in conservatism which originally drove him out. Fredericton has built a statue to him, and he has given much to Fredericton, but no part of New Brunswick would ever have given a man like Max Aitken a chance to succeed on his own terms. *The Daily Express* could not compete in Fredericton with *The Gleaner,* and the average St. John River man, exposed to the *Express,* would wonder why anyone would want to read it at all. The *Express* is tailored deliberately to an incoherent metropolitan society, and its readers know nothing of a life where everyone is everyone else's real neighbour, where banker, barber, professor, cathedral dean and odd-job man, each knowing his exact place, nevertheless feels himself bound to the others within a common coherence.

In a charming essay called *Paddlewheels on the Saint John* (the last river steamer carrying passengers was scrapped in 1946)

Fred W. Phillips of Fredericton describes the life of the river in his boyhood:

"A family excursion to the great exhibitions at Fredericton or Saint John was then an ample reward for a summer's work on the farm. There would be the rising in the half-light of dawn, an excited breakfast and then the seemingly endless wait at the wharf. Finally there would come a long-drawn whistle from 'beyond the point', and in a moment more a gleaming white hull would appear. And those hulls themselves — they breathed the very air of the communities they served. From below decks in those crisp autumn days of the fair excursions came the earthy smells of barrels of new potatoes and fresh apples, of sides of beef and carcasses of pork; and permeating all else, the pungent odour of crackling pitch pine and hot machine oil."

Nobody should ever have called this river the Rhine of America. The Rhine is longer, larger, more dramatic, its banks are crowded with monuments and factory cities, its surface with coal barges and excursion steamers, and its ferocious history has a ghastly tendency to repeat itself from one generation to the next. Those romantic castles which glower at you from Rhenish islands were never beautiful. They housed robbers and torturers, and you can almost feel their wickedness as you pass them by.

But the St. John River knew little wickedness, and apart from small-scale Indian frays in the days when Malicete war parties roamed the river in canoes, the fighting along the St. John has never amounted to more than the ridiculous affair between La Tour and d'Aulnay Charnisay and the so-called Aroostook War of 1839, when neighbouring Maine and New Brunswick lumbermen created an international crisis over cutting rights. Almost the only structures on the St. John islands are hay-barns, and on many of the islands the Malicetes still gather the fiddlehead greens. Only in the Long Reach where the river slants off at right angles northeast from Grand Bay does the St. John resemble any part of the Rhine, nor does it really resemble it here except in width, depth and the form of the hills rising above the water. But the hills of the Long Reach are virgin forests glorious with colours in the fall, while on the Rhine they are terraced vineyards.

The St. John rises in the woods of northern Maine, it curves under the hump of the Laurentian-Atlantic watershed and it reaches New Brunswick at the lower tip of the Madawaska County panhandle. Then it winds through forest country, mostly evergreen, north-easterly to Edmundston, then curves south-easterly down through St. Leonard and Grand Falls and so to Woodstock. From a point in Madawaska County just above the hamlet of Connor, to a point just above Grand Falls, the river forms the boundary with the United States.

These upper reaches of the St. John differ from the lower ones more than Quebec differs from Ontario. More recently settled — the original English population thinned out as it moved upstream from the mouth — the upper St. John is almost entirely French-speaking. Edmundston is as *Canadien* as Trois Rivières, but much rawer and with poorer dwellings, so that the huge church with the aluminum-covered roof dominates it like a castle. French Canadians, no less than the native New Brunswick Acadians, have been steadily moving down the St. John River for a generation and a half.

The river in its upper reaches is slim and graceful, a delicate band through the forests, and it looks quiet until you come to Grand Falls. There, abruptly, you see the power of it. The flume of the falls, utterly savage, hurls itself, twisted by the contour of the rock, into a huge slide of water before it plunges roaring into a gorge with walls more than a hundred and fifty feet high. No salmon could ever surmount the Grand Falls of the St. John, but logs can go down it without serious trouble. Only once in a century of lumbering have the falls been jammed, and then it was done on a bet.

From Woodstock down to Fredericton the river is not much wider than the Thames at Reading, and it flows in bold sweeps and curves. After passing the head of tide at Crock's Point and receiving the Nashwaak, it widens at Fredericton to nearly half a mile, passes under three bridges and proceeds deep and generally still toward the splendid stretches lower down. The Long Reach is one of the fairest sections of river I have ever seen in Canada, and a little below it the stream swells into Grand Bay behind the city of Saint John. Here the Kennebecasis comes in from the east, not as a tributary but as a separate river which ages ago in geologic time flowed in the opposite direction. Below Grand Bay the St. John ends with the biggest surprise on any navigable river in America: it comes to the Reversible Falls between the city and the raw new suburb of Lancaster. When the tide is low, the river descends a gorge with a drop of fifteen feet into the Fundy. But when the huge Fundy tide lifts, salt water surges up the gorge and floods deeply into the river itself. So high is the Fundy tide that ocean-going oil tankers can sail inland when the fall is reversed.

A variable river this, but never a crowded one except when logs come down in the spring drive. Most of the logs these days are cut in the Maine forest near the headwaters and they have an adventurous journey of three hundred miles or more before they reach the plants at the river's mouth. They tumble over Grand Falls, they are shepherded past the Beechwood dam, and finally they come to a stop in a jam three miles long against the great boom stretched between Oromocto Island and the eastern shore by Maugerville. Tugs tow mats of them downstream in barrel booms, and behind the drive come the Wangan boats, which are house-carrying scows powered by outboard motors and crewed by about twenty men. Within three weeks the Wangan boat men clear the river of stray logs all the way from Beechwood to Maugerville, a distance of some two hundred miles. Thereafter the St. John is clear for pleasure craft.

To the selfish, one of the beauties of this river is that so far few American small-boat owners have discovered it; if they did, the stream would be crowded with craft from half the eastern states, for there is no river on the continent more suited to pleasure boats. Above Head of Tide it is too shallow for cabin cruisers, but from Fredericton down to the mouth it is deep enough to carry a ship and quiet enough for a child to be safe on it. A large proportion of people along the St. John own boats, but as the population is small and there is a great length of water, they have most of it to themselves.

The shores float by, the tall grasses are fragrant in the water meadows, ferns and wildflowers blow on the islands, shadows move along the hills. As a picnic party comes round the bend a flock of startled ducks takes to the air, and like sea planes alighting they splash back again after the boat has passed. "Look!" cries a small boy, and there at the water's edge, up-wind, is a deer with big eyes. As the sun sinks, the great hills above the Long Reach cast their shadows over a river violet-dark, and later in Grand Bay, the water shrimp-pink and pastel-grey from reflected cumulus clouds, the yachts becalmed on the flood, the boat party sees the lights of the city which marks the journey's end.

Or perhaps the family turns off into one of the tributaries and camps under trees beside the Oromocto. Or perhaps it goes up the little Jemseg into the lonely expanse of Grand Lake. Or perhaps still another party in canoes is paddling the Nashwaak into the woods where the moose are, or still another is moving up the Tobique where the Atlantic salmon spawn. No matter where you go on the river today you can easily be alone. And if you own a cabin cruiser you can use the St. John as a sally port to any place to which a cabin cruiser can sail. Friends of mine have sailed from Fredericton to Port Arthur in the same boat. They went down the St. John and over the Reversible Falls into the Fundy, then they followed the coastline of New Brunswick, Maine, New Hampshire and Massachusetts to Cape Cod, passed through the canal and so down the American coast to New York. Sailing past the towers of Manhattan they went up the Hudson and then, using a variety of American inland waterways, they reached the St. Lawrence system and sailed through the Great Lakes to the end of them.

Like any North American river the St. John abounds in geese and duck, and wild animals still drink on its shores. Not long ago a moose swam the St. John at Fredericton and spent some time wandering through the city's streets. Deer come out of the woods and eat garden greens as they do everywhere in the Maritimes in closed seasons. But it is in its salmon runs — unless the pessimists are right and the Beechwood Dam has spoiled them — that the St. John is supreme among the fishing rivers of the eastern seaboard.

The salmon in Gaspé, Anticosti, Labrador and Newfoundland, even on the Restigouche and Miramichi, may come upstream in larger runs than they do on the St. John, but there are not so many runs in the course of a season. Cedric Cooper of Fredericton, who has rights on the largest pool in the river, told me that in the St. John there are no fewer than nine salmon runs in the course of a year. The first enters in early May a few weeks after the ice breaks, when the river is so widely flooded that the Maugerville farmers sometimes have to put their cattle in the lofts of their barns. These fish are bound for the Serpentine Branch of the Tobique, where they spawn. The last run enters in November just before the river begins to freeze. So the salmon here are so plentiful that they are exported. If they sell you fresh salmon in the Montreal markets today, they always call it "Gaspé salmon". But not often does the "Gaspé salmon" eaten in Montreal come from any other place but New Brunswick.

"The Saint John is a fine river equal in magnitude to the Connecticut or Hudson", with a harbour at the mouth "accessible at all seasons of the year, never frozen or obstructed by ice."

Such was the first report of the agents of the Loyalists who had come to Annapolis Royal in Nova Scotia in the fall of 1782, had crossed the Fundy and proceeded up the St. John as far as the Oromocto in search of farm land for a desperate people. The Revolutionary War was over in the United States, and the victors were earning the distinction later conferred upon them by the historian Arnold Toynbee, who notes that the Americans were the first people in modern times to expel thousands of men and women of their own race, sharing their own religion and experience, because of their political activities. The president of the Board of Agents for the Loyalists bore one of the most famous names in the State of New York: he was the Reverend Dr. Samuel Seabury.

Americans had of course heard of the St. John long before the Revolution. The river had been established on the map as early as 1604, when Champlain entered it while still a member of DeMonts' expedition. La Tour had built a fort at its mouth in 1635, d'Aulnay Charnisay had taken it from him ten years later, and nine years after that, Charnisay had been displaced by an English expedition operating in the name and authority of Oliver Cromwell. After the fall of Louisbourg a force of two thousand men under Colonel Robert Monckton had arrived at Partridge Island, rebuilt the old French fort and renamed it Fort Frederic. Four years after this a Newburyport merchant had built a post at the river's mouth for burning limestone and for fishing, and through his efforts a small trade was begun in fish, lime, lumber and fur. But no real development of the St. John was attempted before the British forces were defeated in America. When the agents of the Loyalists arrived, the population of the post at the river's mouth was only one hundred and forty-five. A year later the city of Saint John had come into being.

The Loyalists who settled the St. John Valley were proud, indignant men with a bitter sense of wrong, nor had many of them been rich or privileged in the south. A census of the first settlement shows that every trade was represented from lawyer to carpenter and odd-job man. But they belonged to the defeated party. Some had been "inflicted with the Punishment of Tar and Feathers". Some had "sheltered themselves in the Mountains". One had been "Fined, whip'd and Tried for his Life". One had been "Robbed and maimed by the Rebels". Many could prove that "A valuable Dwelling House had been burnt up by a malicious Set of Men." Edward Winslow wrote to his son on June 20, 1783: "The violence and malice of the Rebel Government makes it impossible even to think of joining them again."

It was ever thus after brother has been divided against brother in a civil war, and in the long run the victors probably did the kind thing when they decided to drive the Loyalists out. They felt toward them exactly as the victorious Soviets felt toward the White Russians in the 1920s.

Sir Guy Carleton, still in control of the port of New York, requisitioned transports for an exodus in those days unparalleled. By late November, 1783, more than 35,000 people had been convoyed to Nova Scotia, and the total number reaching Saint John (New Brunswick was then a part of Nova Scotia) was 14,162. Along with the civilians there arrived at Saint John some 3,396 officers, N.C.O.s and privates of the British North American regiments, and the settlers had need of their discipline and team spirit.

"It is, I think, the roughest land I ever saw," wrote one of them. "We are all ordered to land tomorrow, and not a shelter to go under."

But by the year's end the location had been divided into lots, trees had been cut, trimmed and planed, stumps had been burned out, fireplaces built and frames raised. The skeleton of the city of Saint John existed, and with the river and pine forests behind it, the community rapidly grew.

Less than a century after its founding, Saint John was the fourth ship-owning city in the world, and her clippers were famous on all the oceans. One of the most famous lines that ever floated, the White Star, had its birth in Saint John. Had it not been for a disaster, Saint John might well have become the chief city of the Maritime Provinces. But in 1877 the worst fire in Canadian history gutted the city's heart, and in a sense Saint John never fully recovered from it. From the visual standpoint this was a tragedy. Old Saint John must have been beautiful, for all of its principal buildings and dwelling houses were in the splendid style of the first Loyalists. Rebuilt in one of the ugliest periods of architecture known to man, and rebuilt in a hurry, Saint John today is angular red brick and salt-stained clapboard.

But Fredericton, smaller and more secluded, preserves intact
the image of Loyalist New Brunswick. Situated on St. Ann's Point
about ninety miles upstream from the Bay of Fundy, the provincial capital is a mirror of the Loyalist mind. Here, in a Canadian
terrain different from any in England, different again from the
warm fields of Westchester County, eastern Pennsylvania and
New Jersey whence they had set out in Carleton's transports, His
Majesty's loyal Americans erected a living monument to their determination to keep alive on this continent the British Fact.

Fredericton's little Anglican cathedral is an exact replica of St.
Mary's Church in Snettisham in Norfolk; it is also claimed to be
the first cathedral foundation established on British soil since the
Norman Conquest. Fredericton's Legislative Building contains
portraits by Sir Joshua Reynolds of King George III and Queen
Charlotte, the Legislative Library has a copy of the Doomsday
Book. And the bells of Fredericton still chime across this Canadian
river with a sweet English sound.

They kept it alive here, the British Fact in America; they kept
it alive from the end of the eighteenth century until today. But
they are threatened now and they know it.

Just below Fredericton is the new Gagetown camp, the largest
military camp in the Commonwealth, with a permanent troop
concentration seldom under ten thousand, with battle ranges embracing every known kind of terrain but mountains, with soldiers
from all over the nation. "Canada" is moving into the lower St.
John, just as French Canadians have been moving steadily downward from the upper reaches of the river, and the power techniques of modern America are producing electrical energy from
a stream sufficient to supply power for dozens of factories.

"I guess," said an old Frederictonian to me the last time I talked
with him, "I guess I've seen about the last of it. Fredericton may
be the capital of New Brunswick, but so far as I can see it's soon
going to be a suburb of Gagetown. They tell me there are now eight
of these hydro-electric stations in the province. And do you know
what they've got in Gagetown now? They've got *a shopping
centre!*"

He shook his head, and I thought again of the legendary English
remittance man who stayed here because this was a gentleman's
country, his notion of a gentleman being a man who did not work

in a factory or shop, but had all the fishing and shooting he wanted at his door, and no boss to tell him he could not afford to enjoy it except on Saturday afternoons. I thought again of those old days — I myself am old enough to remember the last of them — when the farm people went up and down the river with the paddle-wheels of the steamboats chunking, and everyone knew everyone else, and there was no confusing knowledge of psychiatry, and sin was sin and churches were not semi-theatres.

It had to go, of course; the old order had to change or rot. But along the St. John a growing boy can still experience the simple things, and learn without thinking the fabric of a coherent society. The great salmon, firm from the cold Atlantic, brace themselves against the currents at the pools, the geese and duck come and go with the seasons, the moose and deer haunt the forests which Charles G. D. Roberts described so well.

"A lovely river," the old man said. "A lovely, lovely river!"

L'Envoi

I have come to the end of my rivers and I don't like leaving them: they taught me much and they gave me rare pleasure. Now I remember the journey out of the Mackenzie country and back to Montreal.

It was only after darkness fell that the total emptiness of the Territories became conclusively apparent. Not a single light shone up out of that space for hours. I talked with the prospector beside me. I went up front to pass the time with a student returning from a summer job at Inuvik, but whenever I looked out the window of the plane there was nothing.

Darkness over the Athabaska and no lights; darkness over the bush prairie and no lights. And then, between eleven o'clock and midnight, suddenly there appeared over the southern horizon a magic carpet of green, scarlet and gold, with some strange-looking flares closer at hand. These were the street lights and Neon signs of Edmonton, and the flares were from the refineries just north of the city. Eight hours from the Mackenzie delta to here.

Late the next morning I took off from Edmonton and flew home across central Canada, losing three hours of daylight because we were travelling against the time-zones. As we crossed the delta of the Red the sun sank into the prairie in scarlet and gold and the channels of the Red through the delta were rose-pink. A quick twilight and then darkness. With the Lake of the Woods behind us, no lights in the Shield. On into the dark across Lake Superior and then – brilliant, startling and small – the diamond-pattern of Sault-Sainte-Marie. Staring down I saw the riding lights of a dozen ships lined up at the docks, then darkness again, a smaller light-diamond shining up from Blind River, then darkness over Georgian Bay. The descent to Toronto, a scatter of lights merging into a mighty blaze. A wait of twenty minutes, then an hour and a half over carpets of light to Dorval in Laurentia, the airport only a few miles from the point whence the canoe brigades had set out for Grand Portage, the Saskatchewan and the Athabaska. It was past midnight when I got home, let myself into my apartment and went to bed.

Falling asleep that night, I realized that if my ultimate destination had been Canada's most easterly city, St. John's in Newfoundland, it would take a Viscount aircraft another seven hours to carry me there, stopping en route at Moncton, Halifax and Sydney. I thought, as I have often done since: "Can we do it?"

For that is still one of the most important questions we have to answer here. Is it possible for so few people to meet the challenge of this vastness and mystery, of this variety of the land where we live because the network of its rivers enabled a handful of explorers to claim it for us? Are their successors staunch and bold enough, intelligent, inventive and creative enough, to merit survival between the two giants — the warm, human, beckoning United States and the cold, inhuman, enigmatic North? Is it old-fashioned to assume that this kind of survival matters any more? Is it unreal to believe that people can love an eternal question-mark? Or does the question-mark, perhaps, answer that latter query? For surely it is true that so long as the fate of a person or a nation is still in doubt, that person or nation is alive and real. It is only of the dead that no questions are asked.

Date Due